Awakening to Your Soulmate
A Decision to Be *IN* Love

John Leadem, LCSW
Elaine Leadem, LCSW

Awakening to Your Soulmate
A Decision to Be *IN* Love
Copyright © 2015
John & Elaine Leadem

ALL RIGHTS RESERVED

No portion of this publication may be reproduced, stored in any electronic system, or transmitted in any form or by any means, electronic, mechanical, photocopy, recording, or otherwise, without written permission from the author. Brief quotations may be used in literary reviews.

ISBN: 978-0983541585
First printing: January 2015

FOR INFORMATION CONTACT:
John Leadem
668 Commons Way
Building I
Toms River, NJ 08755
732-797-1444

Please visit our website at
www.leademcounseling.com.
Online ordering is available for this and other products as well.

Dedication

....

We joyfully dedicate this book to the couples who have allowed us to walk beside them when they were lost.

Contents

....

Welcome		i
1	**A Decision to Try Something Different**	1
	What it Means to Fall Out of Love	2
	Harry and Sally's Story	2
	50/50 May Not Be Equal	5
	Gravity Is Not the Problem	6
	Time Does Not Heal All Wounds	7
	No Harm in Looking at the Menu	9
	OUT or *IN*, the Choice is Yours	10
2	**It All Begins with A Story**	13
3	**Four Building Blocks Essential to Being *IN* Love**	35
	Preparing the Site for the Foundation	38
	Janet and Bill's Story	38
4	**Mutual Consent – The First Building Block**	41
	Not Everyone Looking for Help Wants It	45
	An Uncommon Bond	46
	Henry and Ruth's Story	46
	Evacuation Notice	48
	Abby and Paul's Story	49
	The Way We Were	51
	Drew and Rebecca's Story	51
	One *IN*, One Out	54
	Jackie and Joe's Story	54
	Got Romance?	56

	Our Consent to Be *IN*	60
	Labor of Love (LOL)	61
	Count Me *IN* LOL	61
	Introduction	62
	Challenges	63
	Plan of Strategies	63
	Promise of Aid	64
	Closing	64
	LOL- Count Me *IN*	66
5	**Safety – The Second Building Block**	**69**
	Why Can Romantic Trust Get Tough Over Time?	70
	Sam and Jen's Story	70
	Deeper Wounding	73
	Brenda and Ray's Story	74
	Safety Is a Highly Personal Matter	76
	Roy and Mara's Story	76
	You Should Be Concerned If You Are Concerned	80
	Sarah and Ralph's Story	81
	Perceived Safety	85
	Historical Threats	86
	Current Threats	86
	Ron and Linda's Story	87
	Future or Prospective Threats	88
	LOL- Understanding Your Safety Threats	89
	Joint Safety Plan	92
	LOL- Joint Safety Plan	93
6	**Self-care – The Third Building Block**	**95**
	I Am Responsible	96
	The Blame Game	99

	On Your Mark, Get Set…	103
	The Only Way to Change Is to Change	108
	Tearing Up Your IOUs	110
	LOL- Tearing Up Your IOUs	112
	Ready to Care	113
	My Self-care Plan	113
	LOL- My Self-care Plan	115
7	**Emotional Bonding – The Fourth Building Block**	**117**
	Responsible To…	118
	Mary Jane and Robert's Story	118
	Romantic Hopes & Dreams	122
	LOL- Letter of Romantic Hopes & Dreams	125
8	**Tools for Emotional Bonding**	**127**
	Mutual Support	128
	Support Takes Time	128
	Got Hugs?	129
	Shared Accountability	130
	We Always Hurt the Ones We Love	131
	Finding a Great Accountability Partner	133
	Mutual Check-*IN*	133
	LOL- Mutual Check-*IN*	135
	Reciprocal *IN*put	136
	Input Is Intended to Be Constructive	136
	Critical Ingredients	137
	Daily Connection	140
	George and Jane's Story	141
	LOL- $5^{2 \, (Couple)}$	144
Closing		**145**

Welcome

"What God has joined together let no man put asunder!"

Our family and dear friends who witnessed our wedding ceremony heard the good pastor loud and clear and not so much as a peep of disapproval or doubt drifted up to the altar. When it came to our friends, we understood the silence wasn't so much because they had faith in God's handiwork. In fact, our family members would have been outraged to learn of the mental wagering going on in the pews.

Our dearest friends knew what our family did not, that neither of us had ever kept a romantic commitment to anyone. We were runners who had sprinted away from every romantic commitment we'd ever made. They had heard each of us declare many times before that commitment was synonymous with confinement. Many of them were thinking it would never last. They were not wishing us failure. They were fearful of it.

So was John, it turns out. After agreeing to "love, honor, and obey," we were ready to share our personal poetic commitments to each other — or at least Elaine was. She had prepared a beautiful poem, which spoke of integrity, support and a lasting bond between soulmates. John, on the other hand, had forgotten our agreement to add our personal vows to the ceremony, so instead he introduced a spontaneous promise:

> "Elaine, I can not promise that I will stay married to you ... because I have never remained committed to anything or anyone except sobriety ... I can promise that I will work as hard on our romance as I have on the sober life-style I have built for myself..."

We could only imagine the stir it would have caused in the audience had John's microphone been working. We are sure the priest only heard John's opening line, because he was stunned and began coughing uncontrollably until John was finished. Elaine knew John was speaking from his heart as he spoke about his fear of commitment rather than his pledge to honor it.

The irony of being married on the eve of the bicentennial of our country's Declaration of Independence is close to perfect. For us it was more like a declaration of dependence. The idea of "two becoming one" seemed more like a prophetic warning about what each of us was going to lose. It took us some time and a fair amount of courage, but by working to be *IN* rather than independent we have ended up gaining so much more than we feared we would lose. You will read in our story why.

Over the past 40 years, couples have come to us in various states of romantic disrepair. Many were afraid they were no longer in love, or that their love was fading and would not last. We have greeted them with open arms and a promise of hope that has emerged from the work we were guided to undertake on our own relationship. We want to share with you the same message our clients have received about the direction to take when the romantic luster is fading.

We have been where you are headed, as we once had to make a conscious decision to be *IN* Love.

Awakening to Your Soulmate: A Decision to Be *IN* Love is part memoir, part case study and a great many parts of experience, strength and hope drawn from our work with couples over the years. We spent considerable time choosing a title that speaks in some unique way to each of you. We wanted to choose a title that readers would have a personal understanding of in the same way that works of art are seen differently by each person viewing them – uniquely yet universally.

This book is meant to stand alone as a resource for you and your partner to enhance your level of communication and emotional bonding. We expect it will promote the start of healing the injuries you and you partner may have inflicted on the romance. It is not intended to replace professional help. So, if you need more help please get it. If we can help, let us know.

~ Elaine & John ~

1

A Decision to Try Something Different

Change requires a decision to change followed by action; it requires getting IN

• • • • • • • • • • • • • • • •

If you are wondering what happened to the magic in your romance or marriage, then there is still hope! Feeling afraid of losing love or romance is *good* news. Your fear means you have not lost the desire to be loved and to share love. Your sense of loss or longing suggests you once had a partner who excited you, and a relationship that held the promise of a strong future together. It is likely your relationship began with a conviction the union would withstand the challenges that the seas of life presented.

What it means to fall out of love

....

You are not alone. Troubled romantic couples often come to us knowing there is love between them. The problem, they claim, is that one or both of them no longer feels in love.

Harry and Sally

This was precisely the case for Harry, who showed up at our office feeling distraught. He told us with agitation and fear that he was falling out of love with Sally, his wife of twelve years, and falling into love with his secretary.

"I will always love my wife no matter what happens," he proclaimed. But as the years had passed and life had presented challenges, he found himself growing more and more distant from her. Then one day he formed a friendship with his secretary. She was easy and natural to talk to. As he began to talk more with her he began to confide in her, becoming more intimate, because she really understood everything he was up against in his life. For one thing, she never got angry with him, whereas he and Sally seemed to argue all the time.

The fact that he no longer felt romance, excitement and potential in his marriage – that is, no longer felt "in love" with Sally – was frightening to him. He did not want to betray her and threaten the family structure that offered his children great security. For five years, he tried every trick in the book to block the desire he felt for his secretary and recommit to his marriage. He made efforts to have date nights and vacations to exotic getaways. But his desire for his secretary was unyielding, and he was sure he would finally give into it. He had come to believe he was destined to be with her instead of his wife. By the time he came to us, he was depressed and felt hopeless to make a change.

Like so many others who struggle with infidelity, Harry described his dilemma as if some force was at work within him, undermining his marriage and leading him to stray into the arms of another woman. He did not propose the force was evil or alien, but he was sure he was not in control of his own emotions or behaviors.

Life looks so different through the eyes of romantic innocence, when the maintenance of attraction seems effortless. Things are easier in the beginning for a great many reasons. And many romances begin with two people openly or secretly vowing to be different from the troubled relationships they witnessed in their childhoods, or personally experienced in the past. Such passionate determination creates a bond that shows great promise.

With time our steadfast resolve begins to fade, and most of us experience the weakening of connection with our romantic partners. Like Harry, we see it as beyond our control. We place blame on, for instance, the demands of home, career and family. Or, despite not wanting it to happen, we believe it as inevitable and attempt to lower our expectations of our relationship. Unfortunately, far too many of us view it as a sign we have chosen the wrong partner, and start admiring the grass on the other side of the fence.

No matter how much we rationalize, we cannot adequately dull the pain of the lost romance. It hurts to accept less than what we had.

A Google search of the word "love" yields 3.8 billion hits. A community library would not have adequate shelf space to hold every work ever published on the meaning and essence of it. Clearly a great many people have a lot to say on the subject.

We are not going to provide another definition. Nor are we going to tell you how people should behave when they claim to feel love. Sometimes people are possessive and suffocating in the name of love. Sometimes they are so hurt by the rejection of a loved one that they disavow any knowledge of the person and put a line through their name in the book of life. Some will argue that true love should be unconditional; but does that mean we should continue to feel love for partners who beat us? We are pretty sure we cannot craft a definition of love that fits all people and all circumstances.

We *can* craft a definition of being *IN* love, with special emphasis on the word *IN*. Thirty-eight years of experience has taught us that the colors of romance can be restored and the relationship you long for might still be possible. However, bringing it back requires much more than a desire to return to how things were.

Change requires a decision to change followed by action; it requires getting *IN*.

You caught the twist, we hope.

This statement alone may seem overwhelming, because changing yourself to change the relationship requires you to become emotionally vulnerable to your partner. Maybe you are fearful of not being able to remain fully engaged in the relationship you are building. Maybe you are worried that your partner will run from the commitment once you are fully invested in it. Or perhaps the idea of vulnerability itself makes you anxious. Again, don't be discouraged. In fact, stop wringing your hands in apprehension so you can use them to draw your partner close to you and allow yourself to be vulnerable.

Harry came to us claiming he "no longer felt in love" with his wife despite knowing he had "feelings of love" for her. Our personal and professional experience shows us that the only difference between Harry's – and many other couple's – feelings of love, and being in love is being *IN*. In the pages ahead, we will explain in detail what it means to be *IN*. For now we must begin where we did with Harry. We must challenge and overturn some of the traditional thoughts about romantic love.

50/50 may not be equal

In 1976, the priest who married us was a big fan of equal partnerships. Before agreeing to perform the ceremony, he insisted on guiding us through prenuptial lessons. Our very first lesson started with the message, "marriage is intended to be a 50/50 partnership in which the duties and responsibilities would be shared equally." He further explained that all conflicts should be resolved through compassionate compromise and emphasized the importance of meeting each other half way on all matters.

This is the most enduring and embedded conviction we see in our work with couples. Our role models taught us this, and it is still a common cultural concept, given credence because it has been passed down several generations.

The thing is, many folks preach it without even understanding what it means. We certainly mean no disrespect but we are not sure the good father – whom we loved and respected greatly – had any idea what he was talking about. He had never been in a romantic relationship. His role models raised him in a generation when couples were supposed to remain married no matter how bad things were. The divorce rates the year we were married had reached an all-time high and yet people were still following the belief in 50/50 partnership.

One of the challenges couples encounter very early in the process of making a decision to be *IN* Love is the notion of how much is expected from each partner in a romance. As far as we are concerned, there is little therapeutic value in having one partner draw a line "half way" in an effort to establish fairness. It might work in a football game, where there is no confusion over the halfway point between goal lines. When it comes to relationships, couples can seldom agree on where the 50-yard line is. Generally, a fight breaks out as soon as one partner declares to the other, "you are not being fair ... you can at least meet me halfway!" Whenever two people draw a line between them, it will need to be crossed by somebody or they will not connect.

Our clients have confirmed for us many times over that healthy relationships are seldom 50/50. A healthy romance often requires one partner to give more than the other. It should just not be the same partner all the time.

Gravity is not the problem

When couples come to us saying they still love each other, but that one or both of them has fallen out of love, they usually believe it is the reason for their troubled relationship. They are surprised when we respond, "NOPE!"

After we affirm that yes, they heard us correctly, and no, we were not making fun of them or their situation; we restate our position.

People do not fall into love the way a person falls into a pit. They become interested in each other for a variety of reasons. In the pursuit of those interests they invest time, energy and increasing amounts of their character or beliefs into the relationship.

Nor do they fall out of love as if falling out of a tree. Either two people were never in love to begin with, or the challenges their relationship has faced left them OUTSIDE of love. This is not the same as falling out of love. It is more like *wandering* out of love.

Gravity has no effect on love.

Needless to say, this explanation leaves many of our clients more confused than when the session began. We guess it is because all of us have been told our entire lives that love is something we are pulled into and out of, as if by gravity. Folks who believe they can fall in and out of love seem to view the process as mysterious and as being outside of their own power or control.

This was Harry's view. The more he shared his story with us, the more it became clear that something else had taken place.

Before Harry's relationship with his secretary developed, he and his wife, Sally had struggled to conceive their daughter, who ended up being born with a complicated birth defect. Their world imploded. Sally lapsed into depression. She withdrew from Harry, and became totally preoccupied with their daughter's wellbeing, despite the fact nothing could be done to repair the problem. Harry escaped by withdrawing into his work.

The two of them had no control over daughter's birth defect. They did have control over the way they each dealt with it, which was to turn to something other than each other for comfort. Their decision to do so might not have been conscious. But they did not drift apart; they wandered apart.

Time does not heal all wounds

If you and your partner have been together for longer than three months than you have probably already behaved in ways you have each found hurtful. At some point in your lives you may also have heard the famous line from the movie *Love Story*, love means never having to say you're sorry. While growing up, you might have learned from your adult role models that time heals all wounds.

The actors in *Love Story* may have gotten away with it, but contrary to what Hollywood has taught us, love does mean having to say you are sorry. Time alone does not heal all wounds. In fact, time can easily make the wounds worse by leading to resentments.

Resentment is not simply anger or hurt over, for instance, your partner failing to call you during the day as promised. Resentment is the re-feeling of past harms. It is bitterness over a perceived or actual injury that one partner believes the other has inflicted on him or her. Resentment involves lack of resolution; otherwise, we would not keep feeling it.

It is the nature of all relationships: Excitement and romance fade because of a lack of connection, which happens when resentments build and are ignored. Partners become afraid it will never be reversed. They withdraw and avoid each other to escape rejection, look for what they need in work, work, and more work, or focus all their energy on tending to the needs of their children and other family members. Or, they obsessively, insistently force a reconnection. Both strategies are apt to increase the degree of separation the partners are experiencing.

This was the case with Harry, when his wife Sally turned away from him in their time of pain. First he withdrew from her and into his work. Then, when he became afraid of losing his marriage, he tried to force romance with date nights and weekend getaways. In each case, he ended up feeling less connected to Sally than before.

In our practice we see many couples scare themselves into denying an injury even exists when it begins to look like the relationship will dissolve over it. It usually makes things worse. The feelings associated with the injuries get buried, and when that happens the feelings surface in other ways, in different situations or in other relationships.

Again, time and denial will not heal romantic injuries. Resentments do not resolve themselves, and fear does not loosen its grip on us unless we actively address them. In fact, resentments are corrosive. As was the case with Harry, they will begin to erode the core of your romance and perhaps the health of your relationship.

If you consider your relationship to be bound up in unhealthy ties of resentment and fear, they will need to be addressed and healing strategies will need to be undertaken. How to do the work will become clear as you and your partner work through your decision to be *IN* Love. For now, let us assure you that even relationships consumed with deep resentment can be rebuilt, including those devastated by betrayal. It requires viewing the resentments as part of the problem, not just the result. Couples who view it as part of the problem end up addressing it cooperatively.

When it came to our own marriage struggles, we needed to share a good many amends with each other to repair a lot of hurt. The same holds true for any relationship injuries. Sally and Harry had to work hard to recover from the injuries they had inflicted on each other over five years. When they spent time addressing their resentments, they were successful at getting *IN*.

No harm in looking at the menu

Sooner or later resentment will give way to the need for partners in a relationship to have love and affection. Or, some partners might venture into seemingly "harmless" flirtations outside of the union, believing in a favorite myth, "there is no harm in looking at the menu as long as you do not place an order."

There is a lot of harm in it. In fact, our personal and professional experience tells us it is the greatest threat to romantic connection. The diversions seldom work to fill the holes in a relationship. And when people admire the grass on the other side of the fence, they end up comparing a real relationship to an imagined one. It generates unfair and potentially harmful comparisons. Real people seldom measure up to fantasy. Even with seemingly harmless flirtations, our partners are sure to drop in rank.

Moreover, folk wisdom that suggests there is no harm in pursuing non-sexual friendships is more folklore than wisdom. Harry's situation is a clear example of this.

Harry avoided turning to his wife over the pain and challenge of their daughter's health problems – that is, he wandered out of love – because sharing with Sally made his pain feel worse. He did not feel the same level of pain talking to his secretary, so it seemed more natural and comforting. He was certain she really understood him. Consequently, he put less and less effort into communicating with Sally, or anyone else for that matter, except his secretary – his "work wife." The more vulnerable he made himself to her, the more he believed he had found a soulmate.

He wandered away from his real love relationship – his marriage – and developed a fantasy love relationship because his work wife seemed so much better for him. In reality she was not sharing the same challenge as him – the pain and challenge of a daughter's health problems. It might have made it easier to share with her. It also meant she could never really be a part of it in the same way as Sally.

The relationship he had with his work wife had replaced the one he had cherished with Sally, because Sally didn't measure up to the fantasy. But his growing romantic attraction to his work wife only served as a Band-Aid for his pain. And the one person on the planet who had a unique ability to truly empathize with him and help him through the challenge was Sally.

Before Harry could reconnect with the romantic love he once felt for Sally, he had to end his relationship with his secretary. It wasn't enough to say he wanted to do so. He had to work at it, and it was not easy. It took a few weeks because he experienced something akin to withdrawal – intense feelings of loss and fear. It took time for him see just how very dysfunctional the relationship had been.

Your movement through this book will introduce you to strategies for being *IN* that will make flirtation unnecessary and infidelity much less of a threat. Please do not resort to flirtation or infidelity until you have tried being *IN*.

OUT or IN, the choice is yours

....

IN Love is a model for romantic health in which the partners, in a committed relationship, work together as a team to build an emotional and spiritual bond. That way each can draw strength from the other when he or she finds his or her individual personal reserves low.

Being out of love – or OUT for short – means that someone is not willing to be emotionally or physically vulnerable to his or her partner. Harry did not see himself as in control of his emotions and behaviors, but if you are OUT, you have *chosen* not to share your inner self (your private thoughts, feelings, insights and experiences) with your partner. It could be you are afraid, or not interested in having that depth of a relationship. Either way, it is because you do not feel safe enough to do so.

A decision to be OUT does not mean the relationship is over, but when one partner remains OUT there will be a greater disconnect. We have found that the partners who remain OUT will eventually lose that "loving feeling" and are likely to discover it on the "other side of the fence." Harry had been sure he could not help being OUT. In reality, the emotions and the challenges he faced every day and concealed from his wife had become too big for him to cope. Once he became willing to address the boiling pot of those dark and painful feelings, it was possible for him to work on different ways of coping.

Changing ourselves to change our relationship requires engagement and investment. You might need to work through past injuries that form the foundation for your current fear, but you will not be alone. If you ask your partner to become vulnerable with you on the journey to becoming *IN*, the strength upon which the two of you draw will be similar to the strength you were given to seek the help you are now undertaking.

That strength, we believe, is a gift from a higher power. Whether you call it the God of your understanding or the collective wisdom of the universe, it is available to all who are looking to live full and prosperous lives. That gift, coupled with your dedication to shared fulfillment, can enable your romantic union to become a source of power greater than either of you can muster individually.

Over the past 38 years, the two of us have learned that romantic relationships can be sustained beyond the honeymoon period when partners work at getting *IN*. Harry and Sally worked hard to recover from the injuries they had inflicted on each other for five years. But they did the work of changing themselves in order to change their relationship. Today they declare it was well worth it. Today they are *IN* Love with each other. Many couples like Harry and Sally have done it, and are thriving in their newfound romance.

2

It All Begins With A Story

When couples share their full stories with each other, they have an opportunity to discover that the tools they use when faced with relationship challenges are causing problems, not solving them

• • • • • • • • • • • • • • • • •

Everyone has their own set of coping "tools" – ways they have learned to handle challenging or emotional situations. The couples we see often have communication problems stemming from the tools they use to cope with feeling hurt or disappointed. Many of these – such as the "silent treatment" – are intended to guard us against emotional vulnerability, and therefore make it more difficult to have a healthy romantic relationship.

When two partners handle relationship problems by becoming less emotionally vulnerable, it comes as no surprise that they end up knowing little about each other's "back story."

Many times throughout the challenges and joys of our own, 38-year marriage, the two of us found ourselves yearning for a deeper emotional and spiritual connection. Fortunately we found it in our relationship every time we went looking for it in earnest. It emerged from our willingness to talk candidly with each other about ourselves.

Coping tools often originate in childhood and adult previous experiences. When couples share their full stories with each other, they have an opportunity to discover that the tools they use when faced with relationship challenges are causing problems, not solving them. They can learn how they might be able to replace the tools to strengthen their relationship.

It takes a lot of transparency to do this. We have chosen to role model for you the degree of openness, by sharing our personal childhood and relationship stories up to the point when we committed ourselves to carrying a message of hope to other couples. Each of us tells our stories separately, in segments, highlighting some of the defining moments in our lives, while overlapping each other's journey.

Our stories contain family dysfunction and some fairly dark incidents that would probably be easier to share if we were sitting at your kitchen table with you. You might not completely identify with them, but it will be helpful to take note of the life experiences that gave rise to some pretty dysfunctional ways we each had of coping with life. You should not have too much trouble spotting how we ended up developing some of the unhealthy romantic tools we needed to change in ourselves.

Our romance has been at the epicenter of greater levels of emotional threat and injury than either of us ever knew prior to our first date. And yet, we celebrate our marriage as the single greatest blessing we have known. How is this so? We discovered that a truly committed romantic relationship could promote greater levels of healing in each other than we would have thought possible on our own. We could not change anything about the history either of us had endured but we were able to help each other change the way we dealt with it.

Individually, we spent years aimlessly searching for our soulmates without success until we realized what should have been obvious. In order to discover a soulmate we needed to journey to the inner being or soul of our romantic partner.

We are going to be candid, and we hope you are not offended by it. We wish to demonstrate that candor is necessary to your decision to be *IN* Love.

It All Begins With A Story

❖ Elaine ❖

Both of our stories, while harrowing at times, are not unusual for adults who have grown up in the "perfect storm" of parental alcoholism. The harm others caused us, combined with our inability to successfully navigate the threatening events surrounding us, had a profound effect on our ability to find fulfillment in our adult lives, especially in romantic relationships. Our role models seemed to mock any effort we made to form healthy attachments. At times they dismissed and ignored us as "too needy." They punished us physically, emotionally and sexually as a twisted way for them to get their needs met. We were left to find love and security any way we could — usually in all the wrong places.

Some people overcome great adversity, and seem to rise to great social or economic heights because of it. They might go on to become hugely successful business or political leaders. However, this does not support the common belief that surviving adversity leads to success. A great many other people who endured tortuously painful childhoods or traumatic adult experiences have not been socially or financially successful. Most are greatly challenged merely to succeed in meeting the necessities of food, clothing and shelter.

It was not much different for John and me. For us, life after childhood was about survival. The emotional and behavioral tools on which we learned to make it through our youth helped us to survive. They also ensured we would always fall short of our ideals and dreams. We were ill equipped to be successful at life or relationships.

We withstood hardship by learning to cope with the pain of our youth. It would be wrong to assume we overcame or benefitted from it. On the contrary. The ways we learned to cope eventually caused more suffering than the threats we had survived.

❖ John ❖

Growing up, Elaine and I tried all the strategies that children who experience parental alcoholism and drug addiction tend to use to cope with seemingly inescapable pain and fear. We hid whiskey bottles and tried to keep secret the awful behavior we observed, to keep one parent from getting into trouble with the other. We tried to do everything perfectly because we were afraid they would lose pride in us. Our mistakes, we believed, caused them to drink or become combative. Depending on what was going on, we remained at their beck and call, or made sure we were "seen and not heard," in order to make them happy and keep them from fighting.

At one time, my dad was prescribed Antabuse to keep him from drinking. I overheard the doctor warn him that he would get violently sick if he drank after taking the drug – and, that it was particularly dangerous to do so given he was a diabetic. I began to put his Antabuse into his bottle of whiskey. I was desperate to prevent him from drinking, and would do anything to stop the fighting that always accompanied a drunk. But the effect of the drug, and the doctor's life threatening warning did not matter.

When this, and scores of other schemes failed, I began to comfort myself by pledging "it will never happen to me"… "my family" … "my marriage is going to be different." I made solemn vows to God, promised the other adults in my family and took blood oaths with my pals in the back alley.

Many children of alcoholics make such pledges. Usually, they only serve as an anesthesia to numb the pain of living in the chaos of the time. My own prayerful ones had a calming effect and eased the pain of living just a bit. But like most painkillers, they were not harmless. Although they drowned out some of the noise coming up from the kitchen, they dulled my self-awareness as well. Then, when I began experimenting with alcohol and other drugs in early adolescence, those same promises helped to obscure the fact that I was becoming just like my Dad. In truth, the pledges were more like self-fulfilling prophecies and played an integral role in my denial system. In time I would see the cost.

Elaine and I carried our pledges with us into adulthood. We continued to promise anyone who would listen that we would never settle for the kind of marriages that had imprisoned our parents. The promise did not ensure true love or help us to achieve romantic success.

❖ Elaine ❖

As a child, I was victimized by, and came to hate, my parents' marriage, as well as the harmful ways they coped with life. And, I was doomed to repeat them. There were no adults in my life with whom I could confide about the alcoholic secrets in our family. In my young adult years, I used tools for getting my emotional needs met that were designed for survival and not for thriving or being successful.

Like John, I vowed before God that I would never drink. I knew I was going to be such a good girl that I would set an example for how my Mom and Dad could live. When, as an adult, I became involved with John, I believed our relationship was going to become a laboratory for experimenting with all the ways to "do it differently." It did become a source of great mutual support and healing. Before it could, we both had to get sober and hit several very low points in our relationship.

❖ John ❖

I grew up in Trenton's Little Italy, where it was commonplace for married men to have a *gomatta* (girlfriend or mistress). There were a good number of families in my neighborhood who shared the same father, and I had one or two friends who came from different parents yet looked very much alike. An elder once mentored me: It was right for a man to be settled and raise a family with a good woman on one side of town; it was also natural to have a woman on the other side of town with whom to have fun and really enjoy life. He spoke as if the mistress was necessary to having a good and lasting marriage. I would like to say this was the only bad romantic advice I have ever received but it was not.

From what I saw, all of the men in my family got married because "it seemed like a good thing to do at the time." The women behaved as though they had learned to replace romance with raising children.

I never expected to settle down and commit to a love relationship because I was strictly a sprinter and not a distance runner. In fact, the only kind of long distance that worked for me in my romantic life was the distance between my partners and me. Literally. I was only able to maintain a long-term relationship when there was a good deal of real estate between me and any woman I let myself care about.

As soon as the sparkle of a romance began to lose its luster – that is, started to require work – I was already in pursuit of my next soulmate. It always seemed that my perfect partner was to be found in the next relationship. It was okay, really, because I fashioned myself a life-long bachelor. Successful romance was a Hollywood creation, as far as I was concerned. Only suckers believed in "love at first sight" and "happily ever after." To me, if you said you were happy and married then you were either a liar or the happiness was coming from an extramarital affair.

By the time Elaine and I got to our wedding day, no loving married couple had provided us with healthy inspiration. I had never experienced a single romantic relationship that I thought would make me happy and fulfilled. None of the many marriages I had observed mirrored what I imagined when I dreamed of love.

❖ Elaine ❖

Neither John nor I are parent bashers. We do not blame our parents for who we are and discourage that defect of character in our clients. In fact, we believe very strongly that good mental health and rich romance requires each of us to take full responsibility for the quality of our own lives. He and I have learned the hard way that we are destined to continue hardship if we believe we can only be whole when others change or repair the damage *they* have inflicted.

We may have thought we knew how to make our marriage different than all the relationships we had studied. We know today that we did not stand much of a chance of avoiding a total reenactment. All we had by way of a plan was a desire and a pledge, and you have already seen how well vows work. We entered the world of romance with quite a few "rocks" in our individual wagons and no healthy tools for making it turn out any differently than the others. So let's have John get on with our "love story."

I will reiterate, even though our families were not our choice for romantic role models, they were not responsible for the romantic problems we caused others and each other.

It All Begins With A Story

❖ John ❖

Culturally, Elaine's and my childhood environments could not have been more different. Elaine was raised in Livingston, New Jersey, a small upper middle class community where the neighborhood children played kick-ball on the cul-de-sac and adults drank cocktails around the barbecue. I grew up in Trenton's Little Italy where the crowded streets were often made impassable by double-parked cars. The back alley kids jumped from rooftop to rooftop in a nearly psychotic game of capture the flag while our parents sat on the front porch drinking whiskey from a jelly jar. I would have thought that a cul-de-sac was a cheap French wine.

But once the streetlights went on and we were summoned inside, we shared the same experiences living with adults who drank too much. In that sense, our upbringing was very much alike. We spent many hours during our courtship relating the harrowing tales of our respective childhood battlefields, and marveled at how similarly each of us had learned to cope with chaos that might not have shown on the surface. It seemed like we had grown up in the same homes.

As a child, Elaine lost herself in novels. She prided herself in knowing that she was reading her way through the public library. She felt looked after by the heroes and heroines she met between the covers of her constant diet of fiction and biographies. I took great pride in graduating from high school without having read a single book, yet lost myself in television. Donna Reed and Father Knows Best were my babysitters, and to this day I am unbeaten at TV trivia from the 60's.

I was obsessed with network families who managed to solve every problem in 30 minutes, including the time taken for commercials. Still, my discomfort was never completely blocked by it, so I gorged myself with food to numb the pain even more. It began when my mom found me crying in my bedroom closet one day, and encouraged me to eat something to make me feel better. She was right about feeling better. It happened almost immediately when I ate the fudge brownie.

I gained so much weight that by the age of nine I was already fantasizing about being a thin kid. I would ache every time I saw my kindergarten picture in the family photo box. I loved the picture because it was taken just before my parents split up for the first time, and because it showed the kid I wanted to be.

At age ten, I rapidly approached 190 pounds and managed to earn the ranking of the second fattest kid in junior high school #2. It was a dubious honor for my "baby fat" as Mom called it. It generated a great deal of shame and anger.

It almost made school as painful a place as home. Except in school there was nowhere to hide — ever! At home I could hide from beatings in the attic closet, alongside my mother's hope chest. I was certain that chest had a dead body in it.

For years I blamed my mom for starting me on the road to a food addiction. The truth is that she only introduced the "solution" to the problem I was having. I was the one who snuck back into the kitchen that night to eat three more brownies.

Elaine had also earned a ranking of sorts. There was a tug-of-war between her appetite and her anxiety, and her appetite lost. That, and her anemia had earned her the nickname of Bonesy throughout her elementary and middle school years.

Elaine and I were an oddly matched pair who managed to find each other. The gaps caused by our social and cultural differences were filled in by the similarities in our emotional and family experiences. We talked for hours about the lessons we had learned growing up in the grip of alcoholism and about the way our parents had failed us despite their very best efforts to not behave like their own parents had.

In particular, there were a great many bonding moments over the ways we had coped with food. We spent hours supporting each other through the memories, and celebrating them as proof of having endured the challenges of our youth. We even reflected somewhat prayerfully that our struggles with weight were blessings in disguise. When you are really obese you cannot do too much and the cool kids do not want to hang out with you. The alienation kept me out of trouble at least until I discovered whiskey. And Elaine's boney structure helped to obscure her feminine shape from the wandering eyes from some – but unfortunately not all – of the sexual predators in her life.

Sharing intimately with each other created a close bond that formed early in our relationship. It provided us with mutual support and personal validation. It was as if we had always known each other.

❖ *Elaine* ❖

My preteen years were a time for intense training for romance and intimate communication – sort of "marriage college" if you will. Like most children, I intently studied my parents to learn how people who "love" each other are expected to behave. The lessons I was offered left me ill prepared to be nurturing as an adult, even if I had managed to keep my prayerful childhood promise to never drink. In their best moments my parents lived like married singles that were engaged to be divorced, and the dark times they created showed me why I should never marry. I did not remain abstinent as I had promised but I did manage to retain all the misinformation I had acquired about love and romance.

When it came to the trauma of abuse, John and I shared the same kind of stories many "forgotten children" of parental alcoholism can recite by heart. John endured supposed lesson after lesson from the spankings his father claimed hurt him more than his son. I endured sexual abuse – including sexual molestation at age nine, at the hands of a dangerous neighbor. When I went to get help, I was not comforted by anyone at all. In fact, when I told my parents, they scolded me for having gone into the woods they had forbidden me from exploring. I ended up feeling responsible and ashamed for what my attacker did.

Our experiences left us growing up with huge holes in our hearts. The memories became a source of the strong attraction we ended up feeling towards each other. Our stories, and the character we developed, were quite alluring, so that a bond formed quickly and seemed to run very deep. Unfortunately, the problem was that the seductive attraction came from having been pretty mangled by life. We had not taken all the steps needed to become un-mangled. We were attracted to each other like moths to a flame, as the saying goes. We all know how it turns out for the moth.

❖ John ❖

By the age of 13 I had already committed the most egregious acts that I had ever witnessed in the shadows of my father's alcoholism. I was 5' 6" tall, weighed 225 pounds, and was depressed most of the time when I discovered sloe gin in the boy's room at the Immaculate Conception church dance. An older boy asked me if I wanted to wipe "that pitiful look" off my face and begin enjoying life.

I asked myself what I was doing as I reached for the brown paper bag containing the bottle. I only vaguely remembered my nightly pledges to abstain from alcohol, which I promptly dismissed as an immature resolution of a child trying to calm his mother's fears. She was afraid I would grow into an alcoholic like her husband and father. My memories and resolution vanished. What mom did not know would not hurt her, I told myself. Besides, I reasoned, I was never going to get as bad as my father.

By the time I left the restroom, one sip – just to see what it felt like – had become ten, and I was off to meet my one true love, wherever she might be on the dance floor. I became like some kind of 60's version of John Travolta, or a contestant on *Dancing With the Stars*. Can you imagine – a short drunken 13-year old who had never danced a step in his life, and whose obesity prevented him from seeing his shoes, with a Saturday Night Fever and a belly full of sloe gin, trying to boogie his way into the heart of the first girl he met?

I was told it was not a pretty sight.

I had no sooner found my one true love when my dream-like state of bliss was interrupted with a scream. It came from the one of the religious sisters chaperoning the dance. In an instant she and another nun were at my side, wearing the full riot gear of SWAT police. At least, that was what their habits looked like, perhaps because of the sloe gin. One good sister sat on my chest while the other struggled with my dance partner, who was trying to gouge my eye out. My best friend told me it was like watching an episode from the 1970s science fiction TV thriller "Twilight Zone". According to others, the evening ended when I cursed the church and told the crowd that God was dead. A priest leading a mob of students chased my friends and me from the church property. I vaguely remember being warned to "never darken the doors of the church again."

The scene at the church dance was my first obvious step toward becoming just like my Dad. Scenes just like it were repeated many times in different ways throughout my active addiction.

That same year I found the girl of my dreams in the lingerie section of the Sears and Roebucks catalogue and it was love at first, second, and third sight. A dual addiction was born. My pursuit of romantic and sexual fulfillment became my second "drug" of choice, right after Southern Comfort. I did not draw a sober breath or entertain an unselfish thought for another five years. My sexual fantasy and self-delusion lasted another three-and-a-half years after sobering up from alcohol and other drugs.

I had a sense I was in trouble. But I told myself that Dad usually drank too much and hurt people. Dad ran around with other women and used me as an alibi to my mother. Dad was the problem – not me! I was supposed to be different but the prophecy seemed to be unfolding and I lacked the power to do anything about it. I would end up just like him if I did not change. I had imagined better from myself.

❖ *Elaine* ❖

I don't know if I imagined my life would be different then that of my parents. I only know the volatility and chaos in my home left me feeling defective and hopelessly overpowered. No setting or experience was truly safe, and by the age of seven I had perfected the use of fantasy as a way to disappear. I took every opportunity to wander off physically or mentally. It did not matter whether the story came from the thousands of books I read, or my own imagination while playing with Barbie and Ken dolls, or the pictures I saw in my father's pornography stash.

I lived in a world of fantasy.

I felt like I was flowing down the aisle of St. Philomena's church in my white dress and veil during my first Holy Communion ceremony. Sadly it is the only positive memory I have of that sacred event.

You see, that day my parents were fighting off a hangover after a night of heavy drinking. When we arrived at the church we were met by Sister Maurice. She wanted to start the procession and was angry that I was holding it up by being late once again. My parents blamed our tardiness on my taking too long to get ready. Sister and I both knew the truth, but neither of us was about to talk about it.

She rushed my parents off to their seats and assured me they were good and loving people who never meant any harm. They were only going through tough times, she explained. It was rationalization and denial. When I protested and tried to explain the horrible scene in our living room the night before, she reminded me of the fourth commandment to honor my father and mother. I was silenced.

As I always did at such moments, I quickly departed for the world of fantasy that had become my anesthesia. I knew the Sister was talking and I was impressed by the seriousness of her expressions, but I could no longer hear what she was saying or speak my truth. I guess it was just as well because I did not want to be disrespectful and I do not believe she had the ability to fully embrace the horrors of my home life.

As deeply in love as I was with my childhood understanding of God, as much as I took comfort in my religious education, even church was not a safe place.

The remainder of the communion ceremony was spent in the zone of self-delusion that I would go to again and again in the years to come. I fantasized about being married to my communion partner, with thoughts of living together happily ever after. Pursuing men so that they would rescue me, whether in fantasy or reality, was a theme to which I returned to over and over again throughout my life, until I properly addressed my sex and love addiction.

The following years were marred with the unbearable pain of sexual abuse that, as much as I tried, could not be numbed. Neither my flights of fantasy nor my attempts to assume the lives of the heroes and heroines I read about in the library books could make the world feel right. I needed more.

I found alcohol by age 15. Along with other drugs, the alcohol supercharged my fantastic escapes from reality. I also became secretly engaged the same year, to a 16-year-old boy who worshipped the ground I walked on. I was not exactly sure what the phrase, "worship the ground I walked on," meant but I had heard it while attending marriage college. This love seemed like a remedy for the haunting memories of my sexual abuse six years earlier. I had a new solution that would assure me that I would be safe at last. I figured being worshiped had to be a phenomenon associated with a soulmate.

I wonder if there is a connection between beginning to drink and getting engaged at 15? I am only kidding — of course there was.

I had finally found the love I had longed for and a way to feel that I was always enough no matter how I looked or what my parents or other critics said about me. No, not my fiancée, if that is what you were thinking. I found alcohol, which the bible suggests is a gift from God that "gladdens the heart of men." It was right there all along – right beneath my nose. I guess that I had missed it, I told myself, because I had mistaken it to be the root of all my parent's problems and the trigger for all the chaos in my home. I rationalized that my parents were mentally weak and that is why it brought out the worst in them. But it was going to be different for me.

I defiantly took risks in order to feel good and when that did not work any longer, I found myself going to any lengths necessary to feel nothing at all. By the time I reached high school I had gone from a good little girl who could not understand why others did not see me or treat me that way, to an alcoholic who desperately sought and attempted to conquer every possible suitor – especially the ones that worshiped me. There was no fidelity, no honor, no decency and most of all very little conscience to get in my way. Instead, I was filled with anger at all of the men who had abused me and for the others whom I thought failed to protect and care for me. I was determined to get even with them all no matter what it cost me. Within a year of graduation I found myself at odds with everything and everybody and barely able to come up with one good reason to not take my own life.

Like many adult children of alcoholics, I tried to avoid having my drinking behavior look problematic. I usually sought out marijuana and other available drugs, because it took the edge off the behavior that alcohol seemed to sharpen in me. Besides, everyone claimed marijuana was non-addictive. The reality was that my drinking behavior began to look a bit like the behavior I swore I would never repeat. I was off on another yellow brick road and I was headed to Oz.

❖ John ❖

The drinking and drugging stopped on January 1, 1971. By the grace of God and the self-help group support I receive on a daily basis, that chapter will remain closed.

My entrance into the self-help rooms was nothing out of the ordinary for a typical alcoholic of the early 70's. I had no money, no education, tons of debt, no employable skills, no promise for the future, a small junk yard of damaged autos and a huge wake of broken hearts and promises. The only difference between me and the other alcoholics I met was that I was 18 and the average age in the meetings at the time was 60 years old.

Recovering alcoholics are often heard to share that "my worse day sober is better than my best day drinking." It is a self-reminder that no matter how bad things look, life before sobriety was more intolerable. That was not true for me. Some of my sober days were worse than my worst days drinking because I really had two addictions and I had only addressed one. My imperious pursuit of love and romance did not stop when I put the cork in the jug. In fact, it intensified into a reign of terror that would have led to my getting kicked out of the recovery culture if the groups had provisions for expelling members.

I sought the answer to my emotional unhappiness and spiritual unrest in romance. And I continued to objectify women while doing so. Most of the amends that I would one day need to make would be grounded in the behavior associated with what, at the time, was called womanizing. I know it today as a love and sex addiction.

It All Begins With A Story

❖ *Elaine* ❖

At the age of 18, I entered a self-help support group to get help for the injuries I had endured during my parents' drinking. I believed I was okay and only needed my parents to stop drinking so my life would be better. I was doubtful, to say the least, that I could ever change, and wasn't too interested in doing so anyway. Regardless, I certainly did not believe I could do this with a room full of strangers promoting the use of tools designed to change me. I was even less trusting of the smiling faces that seemed to show up at every meeting I attended. The wall I had built around myself was one of sarcasm and defiance – no one could help me. I took great pride in being able to take care of myself rather than rely on anyone!

Reliance was a recipe for disaster – or so I thought. Despite attending the self-help meetings I was vehemently opposed to dropping my guard and becoming vulnerable in them. I could not see at the time that my very best efforts to protect myself had failed to insulate me from the injury brought by others or myself.

When I finally dropped my guard, the obsession to use substances to alter my mood was removed early. The relationships I formed in the self-help culture encouraged me and guided me through a series of twelve steps that helped to make a profound change in my personality. The changes made it possible for me to imagine a life without revenge and the prospect of love.

The women in the fellowship became my parents and extended family members. The other young people I met encouraged me to live in union with others rather than at war with everyone and in defiance of the God that I had thought had abandoned me in the woods when I was abused. The folks in the group had similarly suffered the pain of living with, and loving an alcoholic. Some also bore the scars of sexual abuse. It helped me to remain drug free even though that was not the goal of the particular fellowship I first entered.

Unfortunately, I avoided my need to address my personal powerlessness over alcohol, which was still there even though I had managed to stop drinking. That step would not come for many years. I was able to stop short of the acknowledgement that I had turned out just like my alcoholic parents until my untreated love and sex addiction nearly claimed my life.

John and I met in a self-help fellowship and I saw in our relationship an opportunity to rewrite the way the story of my life would end. He was not the perfect man; in fact he openly talked about his flaws. He was certainly not the man that my childhood heroines road off into the sunset with. He did not worship the ground I walked on – heck, he seemed to be whole without me. I recoiled from his claim that, while he loved me, I would always come third in line, after the self-help fellowship he had come to know as family and after his relationship with God, which he claimed was first and foremost. I do not know why I did not run from the relationship immediately; perhaps it was because the people who were helping me had warned me not to leave before the miracle happened or perhaps it was because we were brought together to promote continued healing in each other.

❖ John ❖

My untreated love and sex addiction brought me to a bottom that I had never known with addictive substances. Perhaps it was because I had been sober long enough to know better and besides the havoc I was wreaking could no longer be credited to intoxicants. I had spent three and one-half years shooting romantic fish in the self-help group barrel and my last romantic conquest had tried to kill herself after our breakup that I had fashioned was for her own good.

I feared I had become constitutionally incapable of being honest with others or myself. I confessed my sins to someone to whom many others turned for advice. I told him of my fear. He gave me advice that was both good and bad. The good advice was that there was hope for me because a person who was constitutionally incapable of being honest with himself or others would never pose the question in the first place. Sociopaths, he assured me, don't walk around wondering whether or not they really have a conscience.

The bad advice was two-fold. He told me my problem with women was due to insecurity and an immature desire to allow them to get too close to my personal business. "Romance and love is great," he growled, "but it needs to be kept separate from the business of recovery from alcoholism." He warned that I should never let a loved one meddle in how I lived my life or how I managed my program of recovery from alcoholism. He further encouraged that all was "fair in love and war" and that I would be better off not making any emotional commitments. He closed by reminding me that "under every skirt there was a slip" as if the women themselves would be the reason I might relapse back into active addiction.

In a world of pain with no anesthesia, I sought to retreat in the priesthood. When the priest "recruiter" convinced me that I was trying to run from my problems with women, I entered a period of abstinence from romance and sex. The idea was to find out why my life became so very unmanageable every time I entered a romance.

During the 20-month period of romantic and sexual celibacy I discovered that my desire to fill the hole in my spirit with a romance or with sex was virtually the same strategy I had unsuccessfully attempted with booze. I came to understand the deeper meaning of the phrase that I had heard used by the seasoned members of the alcoholism recovery community, "our liquor was but a symptom". My obsession with women, sex and romance was every bit as addictive as my love affair with Southern Comfort or Devil Dogs had been. The first self-help group for sex addicts was not going to arrive on the scene for another six years. I spent many hours educating the men in my support system about how to help me avoid the imperious urge to pursue romance and sex to fill my emptiness. I needed to learn how to fill the void in me without objectifying a person in an effort to make me feel better.

Nearly two years after entering what I had originally thought was going to be a desert of deprivation, I emerged from the oasis a free man. The work I had undertaken to be rid of my defects of character had revealed that I had used three different things – booze, addictive romance and uncommitted sex – to fill the same emotional and spiritual holes in me. A slip was not to be found under every skirt any more than peace or fulfillment could be secured there. In fact the problem was not the skirts at all. I had been focused only on the unmanageability I had experienced as a result of the addictive substances that I put into my body and skirting my other addictive problems for far too long. My obsession was lifted and I discovered my life long mate when I was not even looking – imagine that.

❖ Elaine ❖

Our courtship lasted nine months before we were married, in the same church where I had fantasized myself as a childhood bride 12 years earlier during my communion.

We exchanged vows and John began his with the statement: "I cannot promise that I will stay married to you because I have never remained committed to anything or anyone but I will promise I will make a lot of noise if I am troubled or unhappy". Father Kaven appeared shocked by John's promise but I understood perfectly well what he meant. He was committed to our marriage despite not yet fully understanding why he always ran from romantic commitment. I wish I had offered the same vow.

Before our first anniversary I had cheated on him, surrendered my abstinence from alcohol and discarded every recovery commitment I had ever made to him, my God and myself. He was aware of my withdrawal from the self-help support groups but not the affair. The affair was not an attempt to free myself from my marriage or an angry vengeful retribution against John. I loved him. It was me who was in trouble.

Our intimate relationship had awakened in me the two-headed demon of anger and fear. As a child I had been very angry for being dependent on my perpetrators. That anger was coaxed to the surface by the interdependency John and I were developing. I had learned fear of vulnerability at the hands of my abuser and other perpetrators throughout my teens. I had come to believe that being dependent meant being weak and vulnerable. I had never imagined that two people could support each other by leaning on each other. I always envisioned that some one would have to be weak and someone would have to be strong and the weak person was going to get hurt.

The closer I got to John, the more my fear screamed, "run for your life!"

I was not at all unique. For people who have experienced trauma, an equal or greater trauma later down the road, or feelings of intense vulnerability experienced in a truly intimate relationship, can trigger post-traumatic memories. That was the case for me. Our closeness brought my memories of traumatic injury to the forefront of my awareness and I felt profoundly unsafe and wildly out of control in much the same way I did as a child.

The demons were in control once more and I experienced a great surge of personal power over the fear when I seduced a coworker until I had successfully reenacted the traumatic abuses of my past. I was horrified by my infidelity and felt such self-loathing after the event that I did not want to live.

Neither of us addressed the distance growing between us prior to and after the secret affair. It was assumed the problems were my issues to address through my program. John attempted to get access to my pain but I held him at bay and his support system referred him to the passage in the alcoholism recovery literature that suggests that "acceptance is the answer to" all his problems. We were close but our programs were not. In this case "acceptance" was contributing to the problems he and I were having.

❖ John ❖

As Elaine mentioned, we were married after a short courtship, but it was long enough for me to receive a warning of what might be coming in our life together. One night, after a tender and loving romantic encounter together, I was awakened by a horrifying scream from Elaine who had just bitten a large hole in my arm. When the shock of the attack subsided and I comforted her though her deep sobbing she told me that she had fallen asleep after our intimate encounter feeling safer than she could ever remember and met up with her abuser in her dreams.

The next day, while waiting for my tetanus shot, I thought to myself that something needed to be done to get her some help whether her program was my business or not. I returned home with a firm resolve to force the issue and found Elaine behaving like nothing had happened. When challenged, she blocked me with a refrain I had heard from her many times before. The past is the past – let it go!

My support group supported her position. I was to mind my own business. Leave her if I wanted but never butt into a partner's plan for sober living. Before the fog of that foreboding night had lifted we were married and giving birth to a very sick child who was not expected to live long enough to celebrate his first birthday. Our lives became consumed with the responsibility for keeping our child alive and a career afloat to pay the astronomical medical bills. Many years passed and we grew closer and closer but never close enough to address the deep traumatic material that lurked in the deeper recesses of Elaine's spirit until her shame and overwhelming desire to drink forced the secret to the surface one Christmas morning.

❖ *Elaine* ❖

John brought me to his lap with the statement that he knew I had something dark to tell him and he wanted to be there for me. He was tired of having secrets, he explained, and my past seemed to be haunting me. Full of fear, I cautioned him that my parish priest had told me the secret was mine to suffer and I needed to take it to the grave. The priest assured me that I did not have the right to tell him about my infidelity in order to relieve my pain. However, I knew that I would not be able to remain in the shadows any longer and I would either need to leave, tell the truth or drink again.

John would say that he was left that morning wondering if anything he knew and loved about me was the truth. He was not sure we would remain together. Despite this, he did feel certain that the answer was to establish and maintain the same kind of emotional health that had supported our efforts to remain sober. He trusted both God and the steps he had taken in order to be free of alcohol and other harmful ways of coping with life. And, he was certain we would be helped by joining together to work through the trauma that seemed intent on consuming us.

It was a terrible time in my life. I had broadened my self-help network years before to include recovering alcoholic women in an effort to avoid a full-blown relapse into the drug-induced unmanageability of my teens. The women in my network supported my mental health and provided the love I needed to remain drug free. I had managed to stay clean and avoid a few close calls with additional betrayals. But I had not done sufficient work on my more resilient defects of character. I had done little to address the impact of my traumatic sexual abuses on my coping strategies and failed to treat my love and sex addiction.

I had a great deal of work to do on myself related to the dark clouds of traumatic memories I had failed to keep at bay. I came to understand, with the help of many who had traveled the road before me, that I also struggled with an untreated sex and love addiction that began in adolescence and continued into my marriage. I suspect John and I would not have had to endure my betrayal had we joined together years before to work on the sexual abuses I had endured as a child. I had been unwilling to trust him with the haunting memories of the many traumatic injuries I endured because those were secrets to be shared with God and a therapist, but not a husband. I had thought he did not have the right to challenge the flimsy reeds of denial and blocking I used to keep the demons at bay.

I was wrong. We shared the same God, children, economic resources and bed. We simply had not had the courage to challenge mainstream thinking which tells us reliance on a romantic partner is unhealthy. We had not had the courage to invite each other into some of the darker recesses of our being. For many years I told myself John would not be able to handle the truth about my betrayal. In reality, I did not want to feel the pain of him knowing the truth. I needed to be willing to let him get that close to my darkness. It was not until that Christmas morning when we were finally willing to be truly *IN* Love.

❖ *Closing* ❖

If your relationship is new and growing we applaud your decision to explore ways of enhancing the depth of your bond. If you have found yourself drawn to the title with a yearning for you and your partner to return to the bond you once shared, then we are honored to have shared our short story with you.

We hope it inspires you and your partner to take the risk needed to explore each other's inner being, because we suspect you just might find your soulmate there. If you are unsatisfied with your romance the way it is; and if you are unsure of what you are looking for; or you are afraid that what you want is not realistic or unavailable… please read on.

3

Four Building Blocks Essential to Being *IN* Love

If marital healing was to occur ... it was going to come at the hands of the person who had caused them the most pain... one another

• • • • • • • • • • • • • • • • •

IN Love is a model for promoting romantic health in which partners in a committed romance work together as a team to build an emotional and spiritual bond. - They are then able to draw strength from the bond when their individual personal reserves are low.

Our work with couples over the past forty years has taken us into every clinical scenario imaginable. We've seen couples who divorced each other three times and were engaged for the fourth; partners engaged in multiple extra-marital affairs; a couple that was determined to remain married even though the husband had a second common law wife and family 1800 miles away; and, a 72-year-old couple who entered alcoholism treatment together to save their marriage.

From time to time we are tempted to write that we have seen it all but that would be naive of us and probably short-sighted. We would probably like to stop being surprised but the surprises keep us young and lately we have needed all the help we can get.

The 72-year-old couple entered residential treatment in the 1980s, at the same facility where John was serving as clinical director. They had recently celebrated their 53rd wedding anniversary but only in ceremony and largely for the pleasure of their children and grandchildren. John remembers interviewing them as prospective admissions, and being moved to break the unwritten rules against family members being treated under the same roof. He approved the admission because it was clear that they were going to need each other's help to unravel the mess that they had made of their lives and their marriage over the previous 35 years of active alcoholism.

John was moved by the fact that they both had only faint glimmers of the love and romance their relationship once had, yet were committed to getting it back. He felt obligated to approve their admission and help them to help each other because they were both so aware they needed each other's support to promote their healing. They had subjected each other to many years of hardship and knew that the greatest possibility for a "booze cure," as they called it, was going to come at the hands of the person who had caused them the most pain.

The wife told John, "My husband knows me better than anyone ever could and if he is honest about what he knows, I will have no choice but to be honest. I need the chance to tell the truth." Her husband echoed the sentiment; "Her drunken affairs have hurt me almost as much as I have hurt her and my kids with my drunken rages. If you will let me help her, there is a chance that this time I can stay sober myself."

The couple taught us a thing or two about commitment and the healing that can be harvested from vulnerable disclosure and healthy mutual dependency. We last saw them on their one-year recovery anniversary. Then they took off to live the remaining years of their lives with their children, who welcomed them back into their homes and hearts.

We remember them in our couples work today as they have served as an inspiration for the model that we are unfolding for you.

The romantic problems caused or worsened by the untreated traumas of childhood sexual abuse and alcoholism are not the norm. You and your partner are not likely to have faced life-threatening challenges such as addiction. And gratefully, most of you are never faced with the burden of digging out from under the avalanche of pain associated with betrayal.

But the principles of *IN* apply just as much to couples whose romance seems to have taken second or third place to career pressures, economic hardships or health challenges to name just a few. We describe some of our more difficult cases – including our own – to convey hope. If it worked for us, it can work for you.

The majority of our couple-clients have remained united. Those who chose to close the door on their romance were able to do so in ways that allowed them to become better friends – in some instances better parents – than they had been partners. We do not assume couples belong together or apart. Fortunately we have generally had the opportunity to restrict our work to couples that wanted to be together. Sadly, we have seen relationships in which partners inflicted so much damage on each other and themselves that they found it impossible to feel safe enough with each other to work toward healing. These couples could not undertake the massive reconstruction project needed to save the marriage. Conversely, we have worked with many couples who were "engaged to be divorced." They decided to work with the remnants of the relationship that had once brought them great joy, and have celebrated many years of healthy romance ever since. Every couple with whom we have had the privilege to work has taught us something about what is needed for the development and maintenance of a healthy romance. The work we undertook on our own relationship taught us that the only way to go was *IN*.

Preparing the site for the foundation

The four building blocks which represent the core of our model for promoting romantic health can be set as the foundation in any relationship in which the partners want to be together and are emotionally secure enough to undertake the work. Even the most challenging couples, who had been suffering for years from mental illness or addiction, have been able to successfully implement our structure and become skillful at using the tools to effect the changes they sought. To illustrate we will introduce you briefly to Janet and Bill.

Janet and Bill

Janet and Bill met in a self-help support group for recovering addicts. It was "love at first sight." Both had long histories of romantic failure that included two previous failed long-term romances for Bill and one divorce for Janet. Because their relationship began when they were both sober, they had both vowed it was going to be different than all the rest. Unfortunately, it was a pledge that both had made many times before.

By the time they came to us, Bill, who had enjoyed ten years of abstinence from marijuana, had relapsed because he was unwilling to address the problems that he had with alcohol. He was struggling to recover from the relapse but not able to stay away from alcohol for longer than two weeks at a time.

Janet, who had withdrawn from support meetings after the birth of their twins, had returned to meetings to find support for Bill. Her own recovery efforts never amounted to more than abstinence followed by minimal support, little or no self-examination, and no real change in the way that she managed the stress or emotional discomfort in her life. In addition to alcoholism, she had a history of depression, which began to flare up after a significant battle with post-partum depression. Prior to marrying Bill, she had attempted suicide and in the last three years of their marriage, she had suffered greatly from sadness, fear and a complete absence of joy.

Bill regretted straying from support meetings after he and Janet had the twins. He acknowledged that he had never gotten to the point in his recovery efforts of making meaningful changes in his character and generally struggled to open up to anyone – especially her. After reading about *IN* Love on our website, Janet gave Bill an ultimatum: Get sober and do the work with her or get a divorce.

This couple had hit the "restart" button so many times they were beginning to lose hope for success. Each had reached the point in which they found themselves afraid to hope at all. Our work with them reinforced for us what we have described in Chapter One. A couple's passionate desire to have a romantic life different from those in their individual pasts was not enough to ensure a lasting change.

So we tried something different. We helped Bill in his efforts to establish and remain sober and provided Janet with the emotional buoyancy she needed to avoid sinking into a dark depression. They fought us every step of the way. They had come to us for help with intimacy and communication problems. Eventually they accepted that getting stable individually was more important then their desire to learn communication tools.

After Bill was able to stay sober for three months and Janet worked on resisting the negative, self-defeating thoughts and behavior that fed her depression, they were ready to begin the work. Once they were stable as individuals, they could take the risk to join together as a team and work to be *IN*. Our model provided them with the hope they needed again. They described it as "a new lease on the life of their marriage." Now they look for opportunities to share their hope with other couples.

Many couples we have introduced to the model are more unstable than Bill and Janet but have been able to enjoy rewarding romantic gains provided they stabilized. While the majority of couples do not require stabilization, the needs differ from one couple to the next. The core requirements of stabilization are that both partners are:

- free of any active addictive disorder
- found not to be dangerous to self or others
- not in need of psychiatric hospitalization and capable of honest and intimate communication
- committed to the relationship as being the exclusive romantic and sexual relationship in both of their lives

If you or your partner cannot confirm that both of you meet the conditions listed above, we would suggest that you not continue using this material together. If you are not certain or have questions related to your particular circumstances, please consult with your physician or a licensed professional therapist before proceeding. If you can safely say that each of you are able to acknowledge that the four bulleted points above describe you then it is time to begin.

4

Mutual Consent
The First Building Block

If romantic partners are going to maintain mutual consent, each will need to take the other partner's safety as seriously as their own

• • • • • • • • • • • • • • • • •

The question you and your partner need to answer from the very beginning is whether or not you both believe it is time for a change – and have agreed to – the level of work needed for bringing back emotional intimacy and communication. One partner cannot order the other to be *IN*. If either of you is fearful of being emotionally honest, or has simply decided against an *IN* relationship, the partner who is on board would be ill advised to try and force it on the other.

We understand if you fear that you or your partner's guardedness represents a lack of commitment that could ultimately undermine the relationship, but please do not pull the ejection cord. There is always a story to explain why a romantic partner would prefer not to be vulnerable, and seems unwilling to be *IN*. If you can get to the backstory than solutions can be developed. We have seen the resistance to emotional intimacy resolved many times in our couples work. It is seldom based on how much one partner cares about the other or is committed to the relationship. The fear and avoidance of emotional intimacy does not guarantee a breakup but failing to address the fear of emotional closeness will ensure that the partners will continue to fight about other more acceptable issues like sex, money or how the children should be raised.

If your partner refuses to be *IN* we understand that you might feel hurt, but please do not try to assert your will through manipulation or retribution. If you force your partner to do the work, you may get your way but it is not likely that he or she will continue to work with the tools we have provided when the pressure is off. Getting access to the story of life experiences that gave rise to the guardedness is what matters. It is there that you will find the key to unlock a partner's secret world of feelings.

For instance, the children who grow up in abusive or emotionally neglectful homes will usually struggle with emotional intimacy as adults. An adult who has learned to cover up his or her emotions because the expression of honest emotions seemed to cause problems in the home is likely to be either emotionally reserved or very controlling. If your partner attributed the hurt she or he endured as a child to the expression of emotion than your pressure for him or her to open up is likely to backfire. You do not want to inflict the same type of emotional injury that probably caused your partner's need for guardedness or resistance to begin with. The work will become bogged down in mistrust if you push where you are not wanted or do not have permission to go.

The decision to remain emotionally detached or guarded is a learned response intended to keep us safe during times of real or assumed threat. Elaine's childhood story is a good example of how a romantic partner might develop a distrust of emotional vulnerability. You'll remember in her story, she was hurt during a time in her life where she believed all people were good and she seemed to be naturally positive and outgoing. When children are emotionally vulnerable in that way and they are betrayed by those who they trust to protect them, they can began to associate openness and hurt as

Mutual Consent – The First Building Block

having a cause/effect relationship. Elaine was not molested because she trusted people. The people who injured her were not to be trusted only she did not know that.

Most of us begin life without such guardedness. We ask questions freely, without wondering if others were going to think we were stupid. We aren't prejudiced. Boys can hug other boys and even their fathers. Little girls and boys can be great friends. They can enjoy moments of great collaboration and bonding before learning gender expectations that dictate how they are to play together. And, the expression of our feelings came naturally and freely. We cried when we were unhappy and we laughed when we saw "magic."

In time each of us learns to adapt to the expectations and behaviors of those around us. If we are told it is stupid to ask questions, then we learn not to ask them. We start to assume we are supposed to know everything about everything. Asking for help is especially out of the question. We learn from our role models and occasionally through experimentation that when we lie about something we have done wrong, it eases the pain we feel over it and gives us a chance to convince ourselves that we are going to make sure that it never happens again.

We are not suggesting you should settle for an emotionally empty or loveless relationship because your partner is blocked up or unwilling to let you *IN*. There are approaches you could use that might inspire him or her to join you in the mirror to examine what is causing the romance to fade.

We are discouraging you from bullying your partner into standing in front of an emotional mirror. It might be too revealing for him or her to endure without professional help. Many times when folks who are emotionally shut down get glimpses of their inner thoughts and feelings, their emotions begin to erupt and they become overwhelmed. If they do not feel safe, they will frequently shut down again in response and they may view you as the cause of their pain.

The last thing you want to do is behave like the oppressive characters in your partner's life who made his or her emotional avoidance necessary in the first place. Likewise, it may not be wise to remain emotionally vulnerable with a partner who is behaving like he or she is OUT. We will highlight that point a little further on in a case illustration. For now, let us caution you that your efforts to remain vulnerable with a partner who has decided that he or she does not want to be open and self-disclosing can eventually hurt you and the relationship. Let's focus on this for a moment before moving on.

If you are in a relationship with someone whose fear of introspection or self-disclosure is blocking him or her from sharing his or her innermost thoughts and feelings, then you will likely become resentful and mistrusting. If you were once able to confide in and draw support from your partner, who now seems unresponsive to your emotional needs, it can be terribly disheartening. If you remain vulnerable without addressing the underlying problems, you can become hardened and withdraw from meaningful interaction with him or her. If you are operating from a place of bitterness and distrust, you are likely to be reminded of other people who were unavailable for you and to whom you gave of yourself and never received very much in return. Once this begins to happen, it may be difficult for you to maintain perspective with your partner.

John recalls:

> There were times in our relationship when Elaine would block my efforts to get to know the emotional parts of her that caused her shame. She did this by avoiding intimate physical contact with me. She was not withholding her affection because she was disinterested in me, found me unappealing or punishing me in some way. It was not that she was trying to keep some truth from me. It was more that she was trying to keep it from herself. The trauma of her sexual abuse left her with haunting memories that were easily triggered by physical intimacy, especially with someone she loved.

> Additionally, when she rejected me, I found myself recalling the painful memories of the rejection I experienced as a fat kid and how invisible I felt in my home as a child. Unfortunately I grew resentful of her unwillingness to share herself with me the way she used to do when we were dating. In turn, my sarcasm and

irritability increased her sense of threat and left her with a desire to be even more guarded around me.

It is not uncommon to find one or both partners avoiding both emotional and physical intimacy when they are trapped in shame or guilt by the secrets they are keeping. Emotional and physical intimacy reduces your ability to conceal the source of your shame. The closer Elaine and I became emotionally, the brighter the spotlights shined on our shame. We needed to both open up further and become vulnerable, or run. We frequently ran. The runs took the form of coldness, faultfinding and long periods of isolation. We had senseless arguments over issues we could not remember a week after we made up. These arguments were usually triggered by the fears we did not know how to address, and were not willing to address if asked directly. During those periods we seldom wanted to change ourselves. What we wanted was for the other person to change.

Not everyone looking for help wants it

We never assume the couples coming to see us to work on communication and emotional intimacy are there for the same reasons; or, that they are even in the relationship by mutual consent. We know you must be thinking, "These guys have got to be kidding." Most of us assume people get married because they want to share their lives with each other, and that people who remain married or in a romantic relationship do so out of mutual consent. However, our experience suggests this is not always the case.

Some couples marry or form a commitment, not because they share a common investment in the relationship or each other, but with ulterior motives. Some couples want to be married because it is expected of them by their culture, or because of their societal status. Some people "tie the knot" because they believe it will force them to settle down and become more responsible in much the same way the young men from our generation were pushed into the military to develop discipline and become real men. Those couples usually fight over one of them being too controlling and treating the other like a child. Imagine that!

An uncommon bond

....

We have seen couples who remain married or involved with a romantic partner for reasons other than love and romance. Their motives have been as varied as the differing levels of consent or commitment that couples present to us. The following is a case in point.

Henry and Ruth

Henry and Ruth came to the office for help with the concerns being their lack of intimacy and their difficulty resolving parenting disagreements. The partners had always viewed intimacy as being synonymous with sex and reported that there had been no intimacy in the relationship for the past 13 months. Emotional intimacy had never really been available to either one of them in their marriage. The problems associated with their parenting arguments were quite involved. Their teenage twin daughters were actively involved in drug abuse and neither partner felt equipped to handle the challenges associated with addiction. The couple had no shared interests, philosophies, passions, or values. Their only bonds were their children, a thirty-year mortgage, having grown up in families that left them starved for affection, and the desire to spare their children the pain of growing up in a joyless family.

Their initial attraction to each other was their shared identification with being throwaway children who were raised by extended family members. Their therapy work together as partners was going to be a long and difficult course once their children were guided out of crisis. Both Henry and Ruth will tell you what they

Mutual Consent – The First Building Block

have often shared with other floundering couples: "We were not in a marriage by mutual consent — it was more like a 'life sentence' that we never thought we would be able to escape let alone learn to grow in."

Ruth could still remember crying herself to sleep the night she sought comfort from her mother over her loveless marriage to Henry. She received only a shaming rebuke. She explained, "Mom sat on the couch in a lifeless pose as I cried and cried about the prospect of raising the twins on my own because I knew I would die if I stayed with Ralph." She remembers her mom offering no words of encouragement or loving support – only a stern look of disapproval and the direction her grandmother had passed onto her: "You made your bed, now lie in it."

Like his wife, Henry felt trapped in a marriage that seemed more like a bad dream he could not seem to wake up from. He would use romantic and sexual fantasy to escape from the emptiness of his marriage to Ruth but prided himself in never betraying his wedding vows.

The couple initially took exception to our presentation that while they may have been legally committed to each other; we viewed them to be more like married singles. Once they understood, they were guided through a two-week long intensive program crafted to create goals for their relationship and identify the strengths and weaknesses each brought to the union. The core of the intensive designed specifically for them was based on the four building blocks we are now describing. Their work together eventually developed a strong healthy bond and a shared value system. They will tell you that they were more romantically healthy than they remember being on their wedding day.

They are still married, but now by choice, and serve as a mentor to other couples struggling to build a romantic life together. The bonds of trust and mutual support have replaced the economic and parental bonds that were holding them together for years. They have since come to understand they were bound together by a common problem and now they have a common solution.

Couples like Henry and Ruth often enter therapy with a claim that they are committed to working on the marriage but generally find other problems are creating obstacles. Those problems need to be addressed before getting to the issues they initially sought help for. Some couples, however, are looking for something different altogether.

Evacuation notice

We will see romantic relationships in which one or both of the partners are looking for a professional to issue an "evacuation notice" on the relationship. They look for someone to set the rules for engagement, and many therapists become trapped in the role of judge as a result. Unfortunately a good number of professionals and clergy believe they have the ability to determine whether a marriage has reached the point of no return, and whether the partners would be better off going their separate ways.

Couples who seek out a therapist's authority like that are probably running with the belief that "all will be well when the marriage is over." We are not suggesting that anyone should tolerate an abusive relationship or even a loveless one. It is our hope that romantic partners work toward a mutual decision to grow together or apart without running from the relationship as if the escape was going to be the solution to all their problems.

Couples like Henry and Ruth can be challenging to work with but not as disheartening as couples who enter therapy with one of them agreeing to get help but secretly looking for support to end the relationship, and the other believing in the possibility of change just because their partner has agreed to it.

Abby and Paul

That was the case for Abby and Paul, who were seen initially to satisfy a court order prior to having their divorce case decided on. They had been married for three years and had an adopted seven-year-old child. We do not normally agree to see such cases but because the judge in their case has a reputation for really caring about married couples we thought we would support his request.

Abby had been married three times before her marriage to Paul, and Paul had been single but involved in numerous romantic, mutually harmful relationships. Abby was pretty clear about her wish to be divorced. According to Paul, she had already begun to rekindle an old romance. According to Abby she was only reaching out to an "old friend" during a very difficult emotional time in which she felt all alone.

Paul maintained from the beginning that he was committed to Abby and did not want a divorce, claiming that it had always been Abby's solution to romantic problems. He confessed that he also had some shame over the fact that their relationship had begun as an affair while she was still married to her last husband.

Four sessions were devoted to exploring each of their histories as well as an in-depth examination of their marriage. When we summed up for them what they had told us, Paul and Abby were deeply moved and all their defensiveness melted in their tears.

Abby had a longstanding history of emotional neglect as a child of a corporate workaholic father and a profoundly depressed mother. It led her to become a rebellious, promiscuous teen. She began a never-ending pursuit of love and affection, which became a source of deep shame and rock bottom self-esteem. To her, it was a better alternative then her fearful belief she would never find true love.

She fit the profile of a woman suffering with untreated love addiction.

As Abby told her story, Paul frequently interrupted to say he identified with much of it. He accepted the recommendation that he end his romantic affair with a co-worker and stop his use of pornography that had been an obsessive indulgence that dated back to his early teens. He was hard pressed to view himself as being addicted to pornography and in flat denial that his co-worker was more than just a sympathetic ear. He argued adamantly that he was not the problem in the marriage. The problem, he was sure, was Abby.

Abby concluded the session by agreeing to pursue individual therapy to address the issues raised and planned to withdraw her petition for a divorce. She abandoned the idea that life with Paul was wrong and accepted that another romance was not the solution.

Paul, on the other hand, withdrew his resistance to a divorce and thought it might be a good idea since Abby, and not him, was never going to change. He stormed from the office and Abby cried for the first time in many years.

Abby and Paul eventually divorced after Paul was caught in multiple affairs during several attempts at reconciliation.

The way we were

Many couples assume that all they need is a little help with communication or empathy to get back to the way they were. This was the case with Drew and Rebecca.

Drew and Rebecca

Drew and Rebecca began their relationship certain they had found true love with each other. Their whirlwind courtship had deposited them at the altar, exchanging wedding vows four months after they met. They were desperate to hold onto to their relationship as a result. Each professed a heartfelt love for the other, but fearfully admitted they hadn't felt "in love" for well over a year.

According to Drew, the wind was out of their relationship's sails before they even returned from their two-week honeymoon, during which they fought constantly. Rebecca began to feel like she had never really known Drew. She found herself journaling day after day about the unhappiness she felt and the belief she had no idea what Drew stood for or what motivated him.

They were career bachelors when they met at a volunteer organization they both supported passionately. Drew remembers, "falling in love with her before she finished her presentation during an annual fund-raiser." The five hours they spent sharing their stories with each other over pots of diner coffee following the meeting felt like the most important five hours of their adult lives.

They had each found a kindred spirit who shared so many common stories that they seemed scripted for each other. They began to date immediately and they were sharing marital fantasies before their first sexual encounter. What they failed to discover until their honeymoon was that they shared very few values and the way that each of them coped with the challenges of life were very different.

Drew suffered from such anxiety that he only left the house for meetings and work, and avoided social interaction. He insisted on making all decisions in an attempt to regulate his anxiety. Rebecca saw his obsessive thinking as a severe control problem. Rebecca, on the other hand, was uncomfortable being alone as a couple, and found time alone with Drew to be very awkward after the first few weeks of their dating. She preferred to share many of their dating experiences with other couples. Drew generally obeyed because he was not able to speak up for himself.

By the time their wedding date arrived both were wondering how the relationship had lasted so long given that each of them was

Mutual Consent – The First Building Block

keenly aware of their incompatibility. Before they could get an answer they were exchanging their vows. On the night they first met, three years ago, they could not take their eyes off each other and they talked through nearly an entire shift of the diner staff. During their first couple's session they struggled to look in the other's direction as each related their mutual unhappiness and disillusionment.

Essentially, what begun as a match made in heaven had quickly deteriorated into a relationship of mutual convenience. Today they share a relationship of mutual support and shared purpose. Every important decision and every emotional and physical encounter occurs by mutual consent.

The depth of character they witnessed in each other's survival of similar childhood injuries drew them together.

When you meet someone who has lived your life and is still alive to talk about it, there can be a powerful attraction. However, the connections we form with kindred spirits are usually not enough to endure a marriage or romance. We don't subscribe to the Freudian notion that we marry our parents, but we do see that people are frequently attracted to partners who could have been family members of theirs.

The problem with the "love at first profoundly honest five-hour conversation" is that we are being attracted to the brokenness we believe a prospective partner has suffered. And while that may not be a bad thing it can be an awful choice. If we are attracted to a partner's brokenness and they have not done any repair work, we might not realize it until we have been hurt or disappointed or until we are returning from the honeymoon.

Our work with couples has taught us that a marriage license or solemn commitment does not necessarily insure that a mutual consent for vulnerability exists. Our insistence that our couples engage in a process of securing mutual consent prior to becoming vulnerable with each other has sometimes been met with great resistance. They claim they have a "right to be heard" no matter what their partner thinks is appropriate. The last words one client, Tony, imposed on his spouse were: "I am your husband and you damned well better listen to me." The next time he and his wife spoke was in the office of her divorce attorney. The reality of an impending divorce frightened the two of them back into therapy. Now they laugh about the times they foolishly obsessed over wanting to get back to the "good old days."

One *IN*, one out

....

Occasionally we meet up with couples in which one of the partners attempts to remain *IN* even though the other has made it clear – by behavior or declaration – that he or she has no intention of emotionally exposing themselves. The partner has decided to be OUT.

Jackie and Joe

This was the case with Jackie and Joe, who had experienced over ten years of open and honest communication in their marriage. When they first came to us, Joe tearfully told us his wife, Jackie, had been withdrawing from emotional contact with him during the past few months. He frequently shared in sessions about the emotional challenges and successes he experienced and was always open to input from Jackie about how she viewed him.

Mutual Consent – The First Building Block

Jackie, on the other hand, reserved sharing of her thoughts, feelings, dreams, and emotional life experiences for her college friend and minister. As their sessions continued Joe began to talk more emphatically about his need for Jackie to be more transparent and emotionally intimate. Jackie countered that it was just not in her nature to be intimate with a man outside of a sexual encounter but that she was perfectly fine with Joe's openness if he needed to behave that way. The couple eventually withdrew from therapy because they did not share any common romantic goals and Jackie was unwilling to have her beliefs challenged.

Three months later Joe re-entered therapy alone because he was becoming incapable of coping with the constant rejection he felt from Jackie. He was thinking about returning to some really problematic behaviors he thought were behind him forever. For Joe, remaining emotionally vulnerable (*IN*) when Jackie was unwilling (*OUT*) had become dangerous for him. We worked closely with him to help him strengthen his self-care plan that we will introduce in Chapter 8. We also helped him and other loved ones to develop an intervention on Jackie to enable her to accept the help she desperately needed for her depression and addiction to painkillers.

Joe is an example of a romantic partner whose determination to carry the romance single handedly caused more emotional pain than he was capable of handling on his own. He had spent so much energy trying to get her to open up that he failed to see how lost he had become.

No one partner can carry the relationship's need for connection for very long before it becomes hazardous to the well being of everyone involved. Joe realized that he could not remain *IN* with Jackie without beginning to develop great emotional and spiritual pain.

Jackie and Joe's story is but one of many that underscore why we insist that our couples work from a position of full mutual consent. Regardless of the level of initial commitment, it is not uncommon to see one or both partners begin the process of being *IN* and hit a point where they are not so sure it was a good idea. If doubt develops do not assume that the model will not work for the two of you. Joe and Jackie discovered that they had to undertake individual change first but they would still be able to support each other.

Got romance?
....

Many couples are slow to acknowledge that their relationship lacks romance. It is as if they believe the relationship will be cursed or doomed to failure if their lack of intimacy is discussed — or, even worse, if one partner admits to being unhappy.

Acknowledging a lack of emotional intimacy does not mean the love has died any more than frequent sex symbolizes a healthy romance. Unhappy does not mean divorce. The stories our couples have brought us has helped to confirm our belief that regular sex is no more an insurance against romantic infidelity than infrequent sexual intimacy is a predictor of it.

We are sure that you will agree with what we have both learned the hard way — romance might be fairly easy in the opening chapters of a new relationship. But it requires ongoing attention and mutual support to thrive during challenging times or after the newness of the relationship begins to fade.

The early days of romance are so easy that many of us mistakenly assume romantic bonds are natural and automatic and require no effort. In fact, many couples fear, as we once did, that the need to

Mutual Consent – The First Building Block

work on their sexual or romantic relationship is a pretty unhealthy sign that they are "falling out of love." While that kind of logic makes for hot dialogue on reality TV shows or in the supermarket tabloids, it makes no sense to us. It sounds like someone is saying you need to replace your engine when the indicator lights call for a tune up or an oil change. Seriously, what are they thinking?

Falling out of love. Just exactly what does that mean? In spite of the fact that our clients describe it as such thousands of times, we are pretty sure it is not like falling out of bed or stepping in quicksand. Couples do not fall out of love. When the "love" has died the cause of death is usually due to one or both partners neglecting the physical, emotional, and spiritual attributes of the relationship. When a romantic relationship is left to live off of the memories of past joy, fond recollections of intimacy, or the fading hope that one day a new spark will ignite the romantic flames again, the relationship will begin to deteriorate. It is similar to failure-to-thrive syndrome.

A nurtured romance will bear the fruit of love. The nurturing process strengthens the bond between two people and promotes deeper levels of communication and vulnerability. It makes more love, and increases the likelihood they will pay more attention to each other and maintain open and intimate lines of communication.

The things partners do not talk about or resolve will eventually undermine their romantic bond. The following are the romantic concerns often brought to us by our clients.

- ☐ My husband used to talk to me for hours about the challenges and accomplishments he was experiencing at work. Nowadays I learn about what is happening to him at work when I overhear his phone conversations with colleagues. I feel unimportant.

- ☐ When we first met, Sally seemed so interested in our cuddle time. Lately she does not even kiss me when we meet up at the end of the day. I guess I have to settle for what I can get. We are both under a lot of stress with our careers and the needs of the children, but I feel pretty undesirable.

- ☐ Harry used to drag me into sporting activities with him saying that I made the game more exciting because he got to share it with me. Now I feel like a football widow and hate it when the season begins. It used to be something we shared and now I feel abandoned. I don't want him to give up his love for the game. I just want to feel the same love and attention as when he wanted me there.

- ☐ Bob is so much more animated around the children than he is when we are alone. When it is just the two of us he seems bored and disinterested — maybe even a little depressed. I guess I should be grateful he is such an awesome father but I miss my best friend and I sometimes get jealous of the way he behaves around the children.

- ☐ The only time I feel really close to my partner is when we are making love, or I should say having sex, because we seem really detached when we are making love. I am starving for attention and want to feel desirable both emotionally and physically.

- ☐ My partner used to be the first person I wanted to share my successes with but lately I do not think he even knows what I am working on. How did we become so disconnected? I am afraid about what is happening to us but I should leave well enough alone and be grateful for what I have. I guess I need to lower my expectations, but I cannot help being afraid. I can recall a time when our relationship was beyond my expectations. What happened?

- ☐ When we met at a charitable function I was attracted to his rich enthusiasm for the cause and his commitment to easing the suffering of those less fortunate than himself. For some time we shared a deep faith in God and the principles of our religion which we passionately followed. We would often share the responsibility for our church community and would spend hours planning for service projects we were once so enthusiastic about. We are still engaged in the service projects but we do not share the passion. We seldom spend prayer and meditation time together and I cannot remember the last personal insight we shared with each other.

☐ My husband seems to spend a good deal of time admiring other women and it is starting to bother me. He claims that he is just admiring beauty and that I am not accepting the aging process and that I am jealous of how those women look. He is right about my dislike for changes that are occurring in me but I am not jealous of how other women look. I long for the time that my husband looked at me that way.

All of these pings of alarm represent the tip of the iceberg. The mass of resentments lying just beneath the surface is undoubtedly greater then what is obvious. The hidden problems or resentments are likely to threaten the romance and collapse the relationship altogether if something is not done about it.

The pings above represent a small sample of the symptoms that arise in a romance to signal that something is wrong. As is true with most symptoms, when you do not explore what is going on beneath the surface, then even if the symptoms disappear or change, the core problems will worsen.

Every relationship has a breaking point at which the alarms of concern stop blaring in the background and the painfully routine verbal battles and emotional conflict all but disappear. Some couples are apt to view the calm as a relief or truce. Unfortunately, the disconnection can often be the prelude to a decision to terminate the relationship or to pursue or act on a new love interest.

If you are dissatisfied with your romance, find yourself missing that "loving feeling", contemplating a non-romantic and non-sexual flirtatious encounter or "emotional affair" (whatever that means) then this is a good time to take action. When the romance deteriorates to this level you will probably find that planning for a regular "date night" or taking a secluded private vacation is going to be too little too late.

It can be difficult to know what to do with a failing romance but the best rule of thumb we can offer is for you to do more than you think is necessary because there are probably more problems than you think there are and working through them is going to take far more time and energy than you think it is going to take.

If you are satisfied with the need for change and prepared to be fully committed to your partner, it is time to make a commitment.

Our consent to be *IN*

Many couples are afraid of establishing or maintaining the level of transparency that *IN* involves. Some will claim they were not raised to be so open. Others tearfully question whether or not it is possible to remain unguarded given the amount of sadness and rejection they have already endured in the relationship. We assure you that you will not be forced to reveal anything about yourself you don't want to, and making a decision to become emotionally transparent will not leave you permanently vulnerable.

Whether you were taught to guard your emotions or have come to believe you were born that way, fear not. You can open and close the windows to your inner self whenever you choose. Besides, deciding to let your partner in does not mean others will be able to see the parts of you that you would prefer to remain private. You are not going to be encouraged to take truth serum or a lie detector test.

Whether we keep the window closed to the secret parts of us or make a decision to let someone know us fully we are likely to imagine that everyone will see the truth. We assure you it does not work that way.

Regardless of the nature of a particular challenge you face, the solution to overcoming it begins with safety. If romantic partners are going to maintain mutual consent, each will need to take the other

Mutual Consent – The First Building Block

partner's safety as seriously as their own. The building block of Safety will be covered in great detail in the next chapter but the question of safety will have to be addressed in a limited way prior to establishing commitments of mutual consent.

The agreement we are proposing will be a demonstration of your commitment to develop your shared honesty and emotional intimacy. Your consent is not intended to be unconditional; therefore, you are not agreeing to remain open and vulnerable if the remaining building blocks are not firmly in place. If you are not sure of what you are consenting to, do not hesitate to review the remaining three building blocks: Safety, Self-Care and Emotional Bonding before preparing your consent.

Labor of Love (LOL)

In just a bit you will be guided through the development of your consent to be *IN* with the help of an LOL. We are not referring to the common element of text-messaging slang but it was cute to get you to think we were headed that way. Our LOL stands for Labor of Love and not Laugh Out Loud, which is probably wise because most couples will not be laughing for a while about the plan we propose. No, we are only trying to scare you. The laughter will come, but first the labors of love.

The LOLs we have included in the model are designed to give you the opportunity to personalize each of the four buildings blocks or to practice a tool for building romantic health.

Count Me *IN* LOL

Count Me *IN*, which follows below, is a consent agreement you and your partner will be invited to prepare before moving on to the second building block. The LOL will have five parts: an introductory statement; a list of the challenges you experience when you are considering consenting to be *IN*; strategies for overcoming the challenges; a promise of aid from your partner – what he or she will do to help you feel initially safe enough to consent to take the journey *IN* together; and lastly a closing statement. Before you begin we will explain each section in a bit more detail.

Introduction

Your introduction to this LOL can be a very personal explanation to your partner of what has motivated you to want to work on building or rebuilding romantic health in the relationship. This is not a place to discuss the problems past or present in the relationship but should focus on the hope that you have for your future together. If you prefer, we have created a sample introduction but encourage you to write your own.

Sample Introduction:

I am grateful for the opportunity for us to get to know each other more fully. While there is no way for either of us to be certain about what it will take for us to join together in body, mind, and spirit, I am ready to begin the process.

I understand that the union we are working toward is not intended for either one of us to surrender our individuality or to be responsible for fixing the other. I am fully aware that each of us is responsible for the quality of our own lives. I expect that the work we will undertake together to become more vulnerable might be uncomfortable at times but I do not expect that I will feel trapped by this commitment.

I appreciate knowing that that I am free to withdraw this consent at any time. I further recognize that a decision to withdraw my consent need only be temporary. I will always have the opportunity to request changes in the behavior of either one of us that will enable me to reinstate my consent and continue our work. I believe that our new partnership will enhance our sense of romance and create an unshakeable bond that will serve as a source of invaluable mutual support to each of us.

> All that we have read has helped me to understand that there will be times when I feel challenged by the honesty and openness we are aiming for and I am aware that our work together could present the following challenges for me

Challenges

A challenge is any emotional or behavioral situation or circumstance that might make it difficult for you to be *IN*. For example you might be afraid your partner will repeat an intimate discussion between the two of you with others. When you describe your challenges take care to frame them so that you can later create an obtainable, measurable strategy to address it. For instance, avoid using challenge statements such as: "I do not know if I will ever be able to trust my husband again given the shameful way he has presented me to his family." When a challenge is constructed that way, little can be devised to address it. By contrast the same challenge can be structured to read: "I do not trust my husband to represent me fairly to his family until he tells them the truth about how poorly he has been treating me the past few years." This challenge is written in a way that invites a number of strategies that can be used, which could raise the wife's trust level to the point of being willing to consent to journey toward *IN*.

Plan of Strategies

The strategies you propose may or may not involve the changes you expect from others. Some strategies will only involve behaviors you need to change in yourself. For example, if you have a challenge that reads: "I find it difficult to consent to being *IN* because I am really afraid that no one, especially my husband, will be able to accept me once the darker sides of my personality are exposed", there is work that you may need to do first. The strategy for that challenge may read: "I am going to address my fear that no one would be able to accept me given my past behaviors, by first confiding in a trusted person who does not have a vested interest in my story." If you tell the story first to a confidant before disclosing to your partner, you can develop the courage through acceptance to open yourself up to your partner and risk the rejection that you fear.

Remember, the strategies you design need to be realistic and measurable. If the woman in the illustration above were to say: "I must learn to love and accept myself before I can expect that others will accept me," it is not likely that she and her husband will undertake the work associated with being *IN* any time soon. The statement, while commonly quoted as a psychological truth, has little value in your work here. Besides we are not even sure what it means let alone how to create strategies to intervene on it.

If you have trouble framing your challenges or the strategies to address them, discuss the situation with a spiritual or professional advisor.

Promise of Aid

This is a statement your partner prepares that describes the aid he or she is prepared to offer to help you remain *IN*. It needs to be realistic and measurable as well. Your partner's support should be clear and related to the challenge. The husband of the woman who fears consent because of his continued contact with his past affair partner and his use of alcoholic beverages is not going to contribute much of any value by agreeing to restrict his relationship with the "other woman" to a friendship and promising not to drink to the point of intoxication. They might be realistic but they certainly are not measurable and not likely to be very comforting to his wife.

Closing

Your closing statement can be a brief summary of what you have discussed thus far or explanation of the lengths you are willing to go to have the work you are undertaking be successful. We have created a sample closing but encourage you to write your own.

Mutual Consent – The First Building Block

Sample Closing:

I commit that I will let you know any time I have difficulty with any aspect of our work together and I will consider getting professional help if we both feel that it is needed.

LOL
Count Me *IN*

Count Me *IN* is your first LOL and represents your commitment to fully join your partner in this relationship. It is where your partner will be able to feel your commitment to him or her and to the health of your romance. The "challenges" you face and the "aid" you need is certain to change over time. This LOL can and should be revised as many times as are needed. This statement of challenges you face or the aid you require is not a measure of the relationship's health – but a testament to your vulnerability.

When you have written out your introduction, challenges and plan of strategies stop and review with your partner so you can make sure your need for aid is clearly understood. Your partner is likely to have some pretty good insights into how he or she can be of service or input about other strategies that you can consider.

Write out your answers or reflections on separate pieces of paper.

Introduction

The following introduction is intended as a brief explanation for why I am consenting to do this work with you and what I hope to come from it.

Challenges

The challenges I may face to being or remaining *IN* are as follows:

Plan of Strategies

My plan for dealing with my challenges (Each challenge should have a corresponding plan to address it):

Mutual Consent – The First Building Block

Promise of Aid

My partner agrees to help me with my challenges in the following ways (Describe clearly what your partner has said that he or she will stop doing or start doing to help you feel safe enough to be *IN*):

Closing

Your closing statement can be a brief summary of what you have discussed thus far or an explanation of the lengths you are wiling to go to have the work you are undertaking be successful.

5

Safety
The Second Building Block

Injuries cannot be ignored, nor can couples solve problems by agreeing to forgive without an understanding of how the wrongs occurred and without a plan for preventing a recurrence

• • • • • • • • • • • • • • • • •

The second essential building block to the foundation of being *IN* is Safety. In fact, even though it is placed in the second slot it is actually the cornerstone to being *IN* Love. We could not place it first because it can be risky to engage in intimate communication and vulnerability without the full consent of both partners, especially if the relationship is fragile. Much like it's architectural namesake, the block of safety is actually the cornerstone and foundation point from which all the other blocks must be adjusted. Without safety there is likely to be limited if any progress even if you and your partner decide to proceed without it.

Why can romantic trust get tough over time?

Why indeed? In the beginning most couples will find it relatively easy to trust each other because they are engaged in all that is new and exciting. And, the neurochemicals in which the brains of new lovers are bathed during courtship have a little something to do with why it is so easy to talk with each other regardless of the subject matter:

- Dopamine (also activated by cocaine and nicotine);
- Norepinephrine (otherwise known as adrenalin – starts us sweating and gets the heart racing);
- Serotonin (one of love's most important chemicals and one that may actually send us temporarily insane);
- Oxytocin (released by both sexes during orgasm and promotes bonding)

New romantic partners generally do not have sufficient history together to generate questions about trust. It is not likely they have formed their union following a period of having been mean or hurtful to each other as friends or acquaintances. So why, you might ask, would either of them have problems trusting?

Even romantic partners with no shared past are likely to encounter problems with trust and safety as the newness of the relationship wears off. The life experiences they begin to share together, such as making a commitment to a 30-year mortgage or managing shared finances, can trigger memories of past emotional challenges or traumatic events that neither of them is all that aware of. The following case demonstrates the point.

Sam and Jen

Sam and Jen were seen for an initial consultation six months after they were married with mutual complaints about incompatibility.

Safety – The Second Building Block

Sam related that he found Jen's continual sickness to be both alarming and a source of growing resentment. Jen was afraid of Sam's reaction to frequent periods of illness, which she admitted were occurring at least one weekend a month since they were married.

Jen was deeply saddened by her suspicion that her decision to marry was misguided. She was fearful that she really did not know who Sam was. She explains that, "before we were married I had known Sam to be the sweetest and most tolerant man I had ever met". She tearfully related that she was never sick a day in the two years before they were married. Now she is shocked that, "he gets so angry when I am sick that he acts like I am choosing it as a way to control him".

Sam related that Jen's weak constitution reminded him of his mother's malingering symptoms of fatigue and arthritis pain that everyone in the family knew were the consequence of her heavy drinking. He described numerous instances in which he and his siblings were punished when Dad came home to find that they had not properly cared for their mother. He angrily shared during the session that "there just was no way to please her or comfort her and when we tried to hide from her never-ending requests, she retaliated with those famous last words of hers: 'you'll see when your father gets home'!"

Jen had spent most of her childhood being sick with one upper respiratory illness after another and remembers that she frequently "felt like a freak of nature". She sobbed when she described the rejection she felt for being a sick kid, and the haunting moments when she imagined that her "weak constitution" was the reason her dad stayed late at work so much. The family doctor attributed Jan's chronic ill health to a "weak constitution" which she interpreted to mean she was not strong enough. She had come to hate that phrase and anyone who used it. When Sam accused her of having a weak constitution, she threw a precious piece of pottery against the kitchen door as Sam stormed out of the house for what she feared was the last time.

Sam and Jen were quick to see the historical connections that we presented to them and understood that both of their reactions were being fueled by awakened life experiences from the past. They left the first session comforted by our perception that their relationship was not a mistake that needed to be reversed and decided from that that they did not need professional help. Unfortunately, they did not hear our message of caution: Insight does not necessarily result in change. Two months after terminating therapy Sam and Jen were back in with the same problem and no solution. The work they had been trying to avoid began in earnest.

Sam and Jen worked hard to help each other address the injuries each of them had suffered in the past. The resentfulness that had troubled each of them for many years eventually lifted.

Their work was challenging at times but not nearly as difficult as it is for partners who have engaged in hurtful behaviors toward each other, behaviors that have threatened physical or emotional safety and compromised trust.

Deeper wounding

Couples that have inflicted repeated emotional injuries or the pain of romantic betrayal on each other will face a much greater challenge with the task of establishing and maintaining romantic health. Many times these partners will be so overwhelmed with the pain they have caused or endured that they will feel powerless to do anything at all. Those who choose not to end the relationship will frequently attempt quick fixes, like geographic relocations, or will wishfully engage in magical thinking that the pain will eventually die down if they just gave it time.

In time a romance will die if the partners attempt to resolve emotional challenges and hurtful behavior by waiting for "time to heal the wounds" or by "kissing and making up" over a romantic dinner or an extravagant vacation. Partners who have felt injured in the relationship are not likely to have an easy time re-kindling or maintaining emotional safety or trust with the offending partner. Injuries cannot be ignored, nor can couples solve problems by agreeing to forgive without an understanding of how the wrongs occurred, and without a plan for preventing a recurrence. Otherwise, things will not really improve. The resentment is likely to fester over time until an emotional explosion occurs about some behavior that does not warrant such a strong reaction.

In more severe cases such as relationships that have been devastated by betrayal or addiction, trust is going to be a pretty rare commodity. These couples are likely to find the idea of trusting romance or each other to be a scary challenge if not an "absurd impossibility". We will illustrate this by giving you a peek into the clients whose relationship and individual lives were turned inside out during an announcement of romantic betrayal.

Brenda and Ray

Ray sat in a dazed state of emotional numbness following a horrifying disclosure by Brenda who related incident after incident of marital infidelity. Brenda collapsed into a fetal position as Ray began to sob. She could not believe that she had so thoroughly violated her partner's trust in her and his sense of emotional safety.

Ray had no thought of what might become of their 20-year marriage or of what would happen to Brenda, who crumbled under the weight of her shame and remorse for having so horribly betrayed her partner and friend. He sobbed like a child who was lost and had given up hope of being rescued. All he could say when asked was, "I don't know what the truth is any more. I don't know what to trust about what we have experienced all these years. Did I make the past 20 years into something other than what it really was? Was it all a lie"? Brenda, in an effort to comfort him, tried to assure Ray that she had always loved him. Ray erupted in a maddening voice to say, "Stop lying — stop talking. Don't tell me you loved me when you walked into the motel room. I did not exist!"

When questioned by a friend about the future of the marriage or if he would ever be able to trust Brenda again, Ray burst into laughter and cackled, "Trust, what the heck is that? What an absurd question. Are you stupid? I don't even know what it means anymore."

Brenda and Ray would survive the announcement and the disclosure process we guided them through. We had a great deal of

Safety – The Second Building Block

personal experience, strength and hope we could share with them. We helped Brenda to be able to explain with honesty and clarity exactly how the betrayals came to occur and what she would be specifically doing about the management of her emotional needs to insure she would never do it to Ray or herself again. Ray learned how to manage the post-traumatic memories he thought would never stop flooding his awareness while he awaited the full disclosure process that Brenda was preparing to deliver.

The process required about seven hours and was painful at times but always emotionally safe. It was much more time than some would have thought was necessary but we knew that the energy invested by all involved would be rewarded many times over. It would be the start of the healing that would continue over time for Brenda and Ray. Brenda's disclosure helped Ray understand that her behavior was the result of a long history of unresolved traumatic injuries that included several instances of sexual abuse she endured as a child. Ray could see that Brenda now knew enough about how it happened and what she would need to continue working on so that he could feel safe as long as she worked on her plan. She made no attempt to blame others for her betrayal and was able to see that there would be a great deal that she could and would need to do to maintain her commitment to not hurt Ray or herself in that way again.

The challenges that you or your partner face when you consider trusting each other must be addressed if your efforts to move forward are going to be successful.

Safety is a highly personal matter

We believe that safety is a personal perception and decision, and in most cases an individual's own responsibility. We do not believe one partner has the right to dismiss or overrule his or her partner's perception of whether or not he or she feels safe enough to become emotionally or physically vulnerable in the relationship. Let us illustrate this point.

Roy and Mara

Roy related that he had sat for an hour on their living room couch as he attempted to comfort Mara during a very emotional conversation they were having about her fear of being sexual with him. She related that she would frequently become overwhelmed with the fear that he would be thinking about other women when she and he were being sexually intimate. When he questioned her further, Mara relayed that the fear was generally triggered during the times that she was being flooded by post-traumatic memories of his sexual betrayal with a mutual friend of theirs.

Roy became agitated about Mara's reference to his betrayal and attempted to introduce the idea that it had been over a year since Mara had discovered his affair and thought that she had had sufficient time to "get over it". He further protested her position that she did not need professional help or support from anyone outside of the marriage. She did not want to "expose her shame " to anyone. After all, she continued, "it was his problem and he was the one who needed to fix things". The conflict that night continued on for weeks until it drove them to discussions about divorce as the

Safety – The Second Building Block

"solution to the problem" and Mara became frightened enough to join Roy in a couples session.

At the start of their first couples session Roy looked for us to back up his belief that, given his outstanding behavior and unquestionable commitment to the relationship, Mara should have been able to move beyond the traumatic reactions by now. Mara, who seemed angrier with herself than with Roy, tearfully stated that she wanted to put it all in the past but that "it would not stay there".

Roy may very well have felt concern about the fact that his wife had experienced little relief from the ghosts of his betrayal but that is not what Mara heard. She heard, "GET OVER IT!"

We believe that, despite his cavalier presentation and bullying tactics, Roy was really concerned for his wife. Her anxiety had become progressively more disabling and every aspect of her life from parenting to career responsibilities was being deeply impacted. He felt afraid and powerless and instead of getting the help he needed, he was getting more and more angry.

From a therapeutic perspective his concern for Mara was understandable. It had been a year with no relief from the significant threat level she had felt since her discovery of his affair. We were additionally concerned that she had resisted his efforts to connect her with other betrayal victims who could support her and help her to normalize the reactions she was having. Prior to the couple's session, she had confided in Roy that she was afraid she was "losing her mind." She was too ashamed to tell her family, who would have offered her two options: "dump the bum" and "you made your bed

– now lie in it". All but one of her friends had moved away years ago, leaving her with just her best friend, and that friend had been her husband's affair partner.

The only self-care she had considered was a daily dose of the angry blasts she mulled over on a blog devoted to the women who love cheaters. Additionally, she had been in denial of the need to examine earlier traumatic events that were intensifying her sense of being unsafe. Mara had grown up in a family terrorized by her father's unyielding rage. She was the victim of considerable bullying throughout school and has struggled with social anxiety since early adolescence.

We understood fully why she would struggle with bouts of severe anxiety, and be unable to develop trust and safety with Roy despite his efforts to make meaningful changes. She avoided addressing any of the sources of her emotional discomfort, or looking at any past traumatic life experiences. It kept her stuck in great emotional pain.

Many betrayal victims will remain in the level of distress Mara experienced for long periods of time. Some will consider addictive substances or behaviors such as overeating or compulsive spending to ease the pain for a time. However, those types of "pain killers" seldom dull the pain completely and generally lead to a great many other problems. The fact that she was unwilling to accept the need for more in-depth support or personal therapy did not mean Mara's sense of threat in her life and need for safety were not justified.

Safety – The Second Building Block

We did not support Roy. Mara was able to determine for herself that she was unsafe, and therefore wasn't ready to work on sexual intimacy in the marriage.

She was eventually able to work up a list of safety conditions that Roy would contract for in order for her to be *IN*. But she couldn't until he made amends for trying to bully her into being emotionally and sexually vulnerable in their relationship.

As therapists we have sometimes had to discourage couples from doing intimate emotional work because we did not believe they were safe enough to undertake it. We needed to insist on a number of therapeutic safeguards. We have never made an effort to talk a partner into being *IN* the relationship against his or her better judgment. However, there have been situations in which we have been unwilling to work on issues with couples who we did not believe to be safe enough with each other.

Mutual safety is especially critical to meaningful therapy and romantic healing when partners are engaged in self-examination and communication outside of the therapy session. Couples need to feel safe with each other outside of therapy yet are frequently too uncomfortable to establish safety boundaries without support.

Most people have known some difficulty with the challenge of developing and maintaining emotional and physical safety boundaries, so do not be discouraged if you find yourself confused about how to define safety for yourself.

Later in this chapter, we will be introducing you to LOLs that we encourage our clients to use when evaluating their own safety. It will guide you through a simple yet honest self-appraisal that can serve as the foundation of the Joint Safety Plan you and your partner will be asked to construct. But before we move on, we encourage you to stop for a moment of shared self-reflection.

We have generally found that, at this point in our work with them, some couples will begin to question whether or not their romance really needs such close attention. Those who consider the question seriously will be apt to redefine the problems they are having and decide that the difficulties they are experiencing are unrelated to their level of emotional intimacy and mutual support. We have heard a good many redefinitions of the problem from "too little money" or "too many child rearing demands" to the position that the romance is in trouble because of ethnic or cultural complications that causes defensiveness and blocks communication.

John once eavesdropped on a conversation between his grandmother and his mom the day after his father broke through the front door in a drunken rage. He had caused the family to flee out the back to safety. His mother was sobbing in desperation when his grandmother started the scolding, "Jackie, the problem is yours to learn how to live with. God knows that I told you no good would come from marrying a man who is part Irish and part German." John's grandmother, God love her, was convinced that their lives would have been different if his mother had married a good Italian man. The problem was his father's untreated alcoholism. No amount of cultural awareness or ethnic matching was going to take care of it.

The strategies you choose to help your ailing romance are really up to you. However, we hope your degree of effort matches the level of need you see in your relationship. It is impossible for us to help you assess the strength and quality of your romantic relationship without spending time with the two of you, but the following profiles may help you to confirm whether or not there is reason for you to be concerned.

You should be concerned if you are concerned

The idea of being safe with one's romantic partner or spouse may seem, to some, to be an overstatement of the obvious. That has not been our experience. Many couples seek therapy together because they have not found a way to resolve their conflicts without being hurtful to one another. They acknowledge they need help to communicate with each other in ways that promote openness and honesty. Yet when we require them to develop a safety contract, they argue that we are overstating the case.

Sarah and Ralph

Sarah and Ralph were one of the first of our client couples to challenge our position that safety and trust were not automatically present in love relationships. They had contacted our offices in a frantic plea for help to save their marriage of 28 years "no matter what the cost". They came to the first session as seasoned combatants who had participated in the training of numerous marriage counselors over the years.

Both partners spoke with fondness about the love they once felt toward each other. Both were certain the other had changed and was no longer responsive to their respective needs. Both blamed the other for changing the rules in the marriage, and for behaving in ways no longer acceptable or warranting of trust and intimacy. Both claimed they wanted to regain that loving feeling, but that they were not sure how to rebuild the trust they had once cherished. Neither partner felt there were any individual personal changes they needed to make. In fact, both were fairly comfortable with their respective roles in the relationship and the general conditions under which they lived.

Let us illustrate those conditions: they had separate bank accounts, went on separate vacations, seldom relied on each other for emotional support, held many secrets from each other and were generally only able to be intimate when they were having sex, which was occurring less and less frequently.

Ralph was the sole income earner in the relationship and Sarah had the responsibility for all the personal and household chores necessary to keep their active lives humming. Ralph and Sarah shared no common friends, and were generally engaged in social and community events with their individual friends two to three days per week.

Ralph and Sarah were determined to save their marriage no matter what the financial cost, but that was as far as their self-sacrifice went. When the cost of intervening on the problems in the relationship required that they move beyond their comfort zone, each of them became resistant. And when asked to re-evaluate the long-standing pattern each employed for dealing with social and emotional issues in their lives, they both dug their heels in.

Our only success with them was to get them to stop arguing and verbally abusing each other, but only in our offices. After four sessions they had formed a strong union and shared a common enemy — us. They had stopped targeting each other as the reason for their individual unhappiness. We were going to become their targets. When Ralph was challenged to examine his chronic overeating, neglect of his health care and his demoralizing behavior toward Sarah, the couple's "targeting system" was activated. They abandoned the time-honored position that the other partner was the one who needed to change and rallied together against us.

Ralph was not going to allow himself to be questioned about any of his issues. Additionally, Sarah was much more comfortable complaining about communication problems and lack of intimacy, than she was with looking at Ralph's seductive behavior in the neighborhood. It seemed to be a core problem in the relationship. He tended to objectify women, just as Sarah's father. But as disturbing Ralph's interest in other women was to her, she simply was not going to address it. She had gained 125 pounds since they were married and did not see herself as worthy of Ralph's physical attention, so she did not believe she had the right to question his interest in other women.

We encouraged Sarah to look for work outside of the home so she wouldn't feel financially obligated to accept Ralph's rages about how "foolish and irresponsible" she was with money. She would not consider this either, telling us she was "entitled to be supported" given the hardships she had to contend with in the marriage. There was the beep indicating the targeting system had locked on and we were going to be eliminated. The couple terminated therapy with a shared position that we "expected too much from people" and that their record of 28 years of monogamy was proof the changes we were encouraging were "unnecessary".

Partners who reserve the right to be hurtful to each other have made their partners the target or blame for their own personal discontent, and are hiding something. Ralph and Sarah were determined to remain married "their way" and perhaps their united front against us should be counted as a therapeutic success. We suspect not. We were the fifth place they had sought help in the last two years. They always sought help for the same problems and agreed on the same solution — end therapy when it called for personal change. Like Ralph and Sarah, romantic partners who dismiss the need for physical and emotional safety are likely to go right on mistreating each other.

Sarah and Ralph were like many couples who conclude they really do not have any reason to be concerned. Some unhappy romantic partners may block out the sadness and concern with anger or denial of the need for a more emotionally intimate relationship.

It is wise to be concerned when people in your life share their concerns for you, your partner or the relationship, regardless of how those concerns are shared with you. Try and refrain from comparing your relationship to those you see around you, or to memories of past relationships you have experienced or observed. Feel free to compare your relationship to the way that you would like it to be.

You have a right to want the feelings that you had for each other in the beginning of the relationship. If others are concerned for the emotional health in your relationship, or if they are just vaguely concerned for something that seems to be missing in your romance, then you should be concerned, too. Many times others are able to see problems that are too uncomfortable for us to face when we look at the relationship in the mirror.

It is all right to have great expectations for your relationship with your romantic partner. Some of your confidants might claim that your unhappiness is coming from unreasonable expectations. They are quick to tell you that you want too much from your partner. When you hear from others that your expectations are too high, stop a moment and examine who is doing the preaching.

Look closely at the messenger's romantic history before you start beating yourself up for wanting more in your romance. He or she is probably in a relationship that you would find unattractive or is likely to have accumulated a series of unsuccessful romances. When John got a 50 on a math test in middle school he did not want to talk to the kids who received 90's. He wanted to compare his test to the students who did not get any correct answers. So it is with relationships. People who are settling for less in their romance are likely to advise you to lower your expectations.

Safety – The Second Building Block

If the qualities you want in a romance include such characteristics as safety, honesty, openness, intimate communication, respectful accountability and the ability to count on your partner for support there is no reason to settle for less.

Simply put, you should be concerned if you are concerned. You and your partner know, for yourselves, whether each of you is happy or fulfilled in your romance. If you are willing to begin developing the tools you will need to get the romance you are looking for, we encourage you to proceed with the following LOL's that will help you assess your safety and develop plans for remaining that way in your relationship.

Perceived safety

Partners need to decide for themselves whether they feel safe. Once that decision is made, it is each partner's responsibility to determine what conditions are needed to promote safety in the romance. Identifying the conditions may not always be that easy, because the feeling of threat may not be solely related to current circumstances.

Perceptions of romantic safety can be influenced by historical, current, future or prospective threats that are both internal and external to the relationship. Simply put, internal threats are those that occur within the relationship, such as the fear you feel when your partner yells at you or behaves in ways you see as dangerous. External threats are the risks outside of the romance that can diminish your sense of safety in your relationship.

To illustrate the point we will return, for a moment to our story. Elaine, as you will recall, was the victim of numerous sexual abuses before our relationship began. In the early days of our romance her employer's daily sexual harassment generally left her emotionally rattled. Her threat level was pretty high by the time she got home. One night, while we were cleaning up after dinner, I walked up behind her for a hug. In a flash she whirled around and accidently broke a glass that she had been holding across my arm. The very real external threats to her safety left her with an imagined threat at home that triggered a post-traumatic reaction.

Historical threats

Historical threats relate to past experiences that made you feel unsafe, such as an abusive childhood home life or an oppressive ex-husband. Feeling memories from those experiences can have a lasting and dramatic impact on your perception of safety with your partner, even when you do not see the connection. For instance, Elaine could jokingly tease John about something he had done as being stupid. John would hear his father mocking his lack of mechanical aptitude and calling him stupid. That simple post-traumatic trigger could lead to a cold war between us that might last for several days.

Current threats

Current threats to safety can be real as in the case of the woman whose spouse screams, "I am so angry with you I wish you were dead"! Threats of this type may not result in actual physical injury but the absence of bruises does not diminish the threat to safety.

Most adults will quickly conclude that escape is critical when the building they are in has caught fire. A burning building presents a clear danger most people can easily identify. It can be a good deal more challenging to know what to do when you feel threatened by the fact that the physical posturing that your spouse has assumed reminds you of a physically abusive parent. The threat level appears extremely high even though there is little likelihood of being physically harmed. Safety threats based on past harms may present as if they were a clear and present danger. That does not mean you should proceed as if there is a reason for feeling unsafe.

When a man says to his wife, "you are just like my mother" there is more going on than meets the eye. Does he mean his wife is behaving just like his mother did to him? Or, that unpleasant memories of how he felt as a child have been triggered by something his wife has said or done? Our experiences with one couple will help to clarify this point.

Ron and Linda

Ron and Linda opened up the session wanting to address the disturbance they experienced during Thanksgiving dinner at Ron's parents' home. Linda's described Ron's mother as sometimes quite oppressive – someone who prefers to be in complete control of every aspect of a family gathering, from appetizer to entertainment. Ron admitted that he finds it challenging to be in his mother's company, especially when she orders his father about, demeaning and criticizing his every action.

Linda related that a silent war broke out between her and Ron when his mother began pushing a second dessert on him following a four-course meal and Linda tried to intervene. Ron felt deeply hurt by Linda's attempt to block him from the only pleasure he ever gained out of a visit to his mother's — chocolate 7-layer cake.

The argument continued when they got buckled up for the long car ride home. Linda recalled feeling frightened of Ron's compulsive over-eating, high blood pressure and borderline diabetes. Ron only remembers being attacked and shamed in front of his entire family and judged Linda's behavior as unforgivable.

The session continued on for some time with both partners convinced that the other was at fault. But by the end, Ron saw that his over-reaction to Linda's attempts to help him to address his health needs came from the feelings of oppression he felt with his mom. Meanwhile, Linda's concerns for life-threatening health risks that Ron was ignoring left her feeling unsafe, and as protective as a mother bear.

Future or prospective threats

Future or prospective safety concerns can have a direct impact on the threat level you feel in situations days or months before a scheduled event. It is not uncommon for adults who are expecting bad news, such as the loss of a job, to begin to look at life as being unpredictable and unsafe. This increased sense of threat and hyper-vigilance causes us to overreact to the actions of those around us, and to sense danger where there is none.

The following LOL highlights some of the questions or prompts used to guide our clients toward a fuller understanding of the ways internal and external threats impact the trust in their romance. We offer them to you to aid you and your partner in identifying your own internal and external threats.

They are separated into three different focal points or perspectives as described above: historical, current and prospective or future safety threats. We have also noted when the material focuses on external or internal threats for your reference when you discuss your safety concerns with your partner.

LOL
Understanding Your Safety Threats

The following tasks will help you and your partner to get to know more about the circumstances that can trigger defensiveness in your communication and damage romantic health. Additionally, your responses will help each of you to see what you will need to include in your Joint Safety Plan.

Write out your answers or reflections on separate pieces of paper for specific review with your partner. Do not trust your answers to memory.

When you have responded to each of the prompts please take about an hour or so to share your writing with each other. Take caution not to blame each other for why you feel or have felt unsafe. However, if you regret the way that you have behaved, please share it with each other and offer your amends.

Historical (External)

Briefly describe any past life experiences, outside of this romantic relationship, that left you feeling physically or emotionally threatened or unsafe.

Briefly describe the ways in which your feeling memories about those experiences have or might negatively impact your sense of safety with your current partner.

Historical (Internal)

Make a list of the times in the past when your partner's behaviors left you feeling physically or emotionally threatened or unsafe and how you coped with it.

Current (External)

Briefly describe any current circumstances, outside of your romance, in which you feel physically or emotionally threatened or unsafe.

Briefly describe the ways in which your feeling memories about those threats have or might negatively impact your sense of safety with your current partner.

Current (Internal)

Briefly describe current circumstances in which you feel physically or emotionally unsafe with your partner. Include examples in which your partner's behavior toward others negatively impacts your feeling of safety. This focus will include times when he or she appears to be dangerous to himself or herself.

Briefly describe how you cope with threatening circumstances or behavior in the relationship.

Future or Prospective (External)

Briefly describe situations or events that could occur during the next 90 days when you might find yourself feeling threatened or unsafe outside of your relationship with your partner.

Briefly describe your plans for coping with those situations or events to reduce your feelings of threat and increase your safety.

Safety – The Second Building Block

Future or Prospective (Internal)

List and briefly describe situations or events that could occur during the next 90 days when you might find yourself feeling threatened or unsafe inside of your relationship with your partner.

Briefly describe your plans for coping with those situations or events to reduce your feelings of threat and increase your safety.

Joint Safety Plan

The safety plan the two of you prepare is not a wish list of every change you would like to see your partner undertake in order to ensure total comfort. It is intended to temporarily or permanently remove or alter any circumstance, behavior, or event, within reason, that represents an obstacle to your ability to risk vulnerability in the relationship.

An in-depth review of the safety plans with a therapist or a spiritual adviser may be helpful. It is fine if the review leads to consensual modifications to any of the points identified; however, they are not intended to be points of negotiation that you bargain away. The *required changes* in your Joint Safety Plan should be considered "deal breakers". The only reason that a required change should be altered or eliminated is if the author believes a change is warranted.

Our clients sometimes find that the deal-breaking safety points might not be necessary three months or a year from the original plan but they are points that must be agreed on by both partners if they plan to actively work on the relationship. In other words, these are the clients' bottom line requirements for being *IN* the relationship. The following LOL is designed to be concise but not limiting. Please include every point that either of you feels is necessary.

Safety – The Second Building Block

LOL
Joint Safety Plan

A Joint Safety Plan is not a legal document and should not be constructed to be iron clad and foolproof. We are not asking you to create a plan that will enable you to catch your partner messing up. The plan is intended to help each of you to help your partner feel safe as you work on building romantic health.

Each of you should make your own copy of a Joint Safety Plan and complete areas under "Required Changes" and "Desired Support". Fixing your initials alongside of each of your partner's entries will be used to indicate your commitment. Be sure that your descriptions are measureable and realistic. Write out your answers or reflections on separate pieces of paper for specific review with your partner. Do not trust your answers to memory.

Required Changes

I have listed the specific changes in behavior below that I require from you in order for me to feel safe enough in our relationship to be vulnerable.

Specific changes from partner to remedy internal threats:

1.
2.
3.

Desired Support

The following external threats identified below can negatively impact my sense of safety in our relationship. I could use your help in the ways that I have described below my list of external threats.

External threats to my sense of safety in our romance:

1.
2.
3.

Support I need from my partner to remedy external threats to my sense of romantic safety:

1.
2.
3.

6

Self-care
The Third Building Block

You are responsible for who you have become and what you will accomplish with your life today and all of your remaining tomorrows

• • • • • • • • • • • • • • • • •

Self-care is the third building block critical to the foundation for being *IN*. The block is intended to help each partner come up with a plan for taking care of his or her physical and emotional needs. The term "self-care" is widely used to refer to activities, practices and attitudes that are engaged in on a regular basis to maintain and enhance a person's health and emotional wellbeing. This is what we mean when we use it here.

The activities of self-care cover a broad spectrum of behaviors ranging from activities for daily living like eating, bathing and grooming to a wide variety of strategies for improving everything from personal health and nutrition to enhancing spiritual well-being.

In order to construct a self-care plan that promotes both personal and romantic health, both you and your partner will need to assume personal responsibility for the quality of your individual lives. There are two major challenges involved in taking responsibility for our emotional wellbeing. First we must stop blaming other people, circumstances and events for our own happiness. Second, and perhaps deserving of the number one position, we must face conflicts in a timely fashion and avoid running unless our lives are in danger.

I am responsible

You have read our personal stories in chapter two, so you already know a bit about the ways we were traumatized as children, and how we later managed to bring a good deal of chaos into the lives of others. We believe that each of us is individually responsible for our thoughts, feelings and actions, and we no longer blame others for who we have become or what we will be able to achieve in the future. Clearly, neither one of us is anywhere close to earning our angel's wings. Yet here we are advocating a philosophy for living that promotes personal responsibility for the way each of us thinks or feels about ourselves. We are asking you to subscribe to the idea that you are responsible for who you have become and what you will accomplish with your life today and all of your remaining tomorrows.

Some of you may think we are either a couple of confused hypocrites with failing memories, or that there is more beneath the surface of this "I am responsible" belief. We freely admit to having been pillars of hypocrisy in the past. We showed people what we believed they were looking for in us and lived by the motto that it is "easier to ask for forgiveness than it is to get permission." Elaine will tell you she survived her young adolescence because of her ability to get others to believe she genuinely needed them and loved them. But she never really trusted anyone or anything, and certainly did not allow herself to love.

And about memory loss — you bet we are experiencing some of that. Fortunately, our problems with recall, for now at least, seem to involve having to return library books the same day we check them out because of discovering that we have already read them, or never being able to find a pair of our reading glasses from the hoard of cheaters stored all over our very small home. Today, we live a fairly transparent life so what you see in us is what you get, and our failing memory has effected neither our awareness of the harms we endured nor the ones that we caused.

Yes, we were deeply injured as children by people who were supposed to love and care for us and we were hurt, at times badly. We also hurt others in the pursuit of selfish personal gain or because we believed we needed to make someone pay for the harms we had endured. Much of our personal growth was blocked by defects in our character like finding some villain from our past to blame for the mistreatment that others suffered at our hands.

The very best our morality and self-awareness could muster was the admission that we "might be somewhat at fault," but we were quick to highlight where others were more to blame. As far as we were concerned, we reacted poorly because either people pushed our buttons, or we were misguided victims of circumstances. We knew our thinking was not unique but we were unaware there was another way to live until we were shown.

Most of us grow up experiencing social and emotional hurt from a variety of sources ranging from social awkwardness to romantic rejection. For the most part we generally learn how to get through those challenges even though they are at times very uncomfortable. Unfortunately, far too many of us have suffered through the emotional traumas associated with physical and emotional abuse and neglect that have not been so easy to overcome.

Some folks are able to write off the harms they endured as "mean acts committed by mean people," whom they choose to never associate with again. We did not have such an easy time dismissing the injuries we endured. The primary obstacle to taking hold of our lives and making our own success seemed to be the resentments we had formed for the people who hurt us, over which we mulled over for years. We actually clung to our resentments as if they were badges of courage and honor. We credited most of the misfortune that came our way to the wrongs the perpetrators in our life had caused us. We behaved like we were stuck at the corner of "bad luck" and "misfortune" and we would remain there until the people who had hurt us made things right. Unfortunately, we did not realize at the time that we would end up suffering almost as much for the way that we clung to our resentments as with did for the original injury.

We spent nearly 30 years of our lives either blaming others for our own shortcomings or trying to forget where we had buried the skeletons of our past as a way of deadening the pain. We eventually learned that neither strategy was effective. Seeing other people as the cause of our unhappiness or lack of success was a philosophy of living that left us like rudderless boats adrift in the sea of life. Rudderless boats will almost always crash or run aground because they have no way of navigating the tides. This faulty thinking, combined with rebellious living, led to devastating consequence. We eventually crashed and sank. It was quite a reconstruction process for each of us.

Elaine will tell you, she could no longer afford the emotional costs of the secrets and lies she used in an attempt to insulate herself from her past. It was not easy for her to fully engage in a process of self-examination and emotional transparency, or in the notion of healthy interdependent relationships. She had begun life as the target of blame by her caregivers for what troubled them. By the time she reached grammar school she had already learned to condemn herself for the chaos caused by others that she could not seem to change.

Like many victims of abuse, she began to act out the role of "the problem" that the adults in her life seemed to have cast her into. Eventually she began to look more like a predator than the prey and had learned to adjust the focus of blame off herself and onto others for the way that she was mistreating them.

In order for her to take control of her life and have a healthier future, she needed a self-care plan with more depth than merely the pretense that she did not need anything or anyone. In order to do this, she, like many of us, needed to embrace the idea that her life was not someone else's fault. She had to stop running from conflict. It was not easy for her, because awareness in and of itself hardly ever results in change. She was going to need to put an end to the blame game.

The blame game

Many of the romantic partners who come to us for therapy initially blame each other for their relationship's lack of romantic health. Each partner might start off by calling the problem poor communication skills, a loss of interest in each other, a lack of intimacy, infrequent sex or the absence of passion or spark. They are quick to offer evidence to support the position that the other partner's behavior has caused them to feel hurt or suffer rejection and that something needs to be done to change the other person.

Generally the finger pointing escalates the tension in the session and often triggers a sense of threat in the relationship. It usually requires only one or two rounds of the blame game to trigger both partners into feeling like each needs to protect themselves from the other. Even if the partners are not particularly combative, things can become argumentative with a few simple accusations preceded by the phrases "always and never." When one partner tells the other that he or she is "never ever there for him or her" or "always choosing career and friends over romantic time" the conversation is not likely to go very well.

When the defensiveness builds up it becomes pretty hard for either partner to step back and reach for a deeper perspective of what is happening between them. Each quickly becomes convinced the other is trying to hurt him or her. They each feel justified in targeting the other as the "cause of the problem," whatever they think it may be. It is common for romantic combatants to intensify a conflict to the point forgetting what the original issue was.

Have you ever done that? Have you ever become so embroiled in an argument with a loved one that you lost sight of where you were going or what the issue was? We certainly have. So what do you do?

You could take that moment of confusion to look at what is motivating your bitterness and defensiveness and then share your feelings and thoughts about it. However, that is not usually what happens.

Targeting your partner can make it quite difficult to turn the spotlight on yourself. It is easier to reach into the clouds for a line like:

> "I am sorry you feel that way. It is clear you do not appreciate the principle behind what I am saying. It is obvious you just want to fight!"
> ~ or ~
> "I am not going to fight with you! I am leaving."

Romantic couples hire us to help them to improve their romantic health, not help one of them to get the upper hand on the other. So, we avoid any talk of the "principle of the thing". Couples who have watched too many reality television shows will usually resist our attempts to guide them back into their own corners of the fighting ring. They believe they have earned the right to be heard, and trust we will rule in their favor. Yet we have found that romantic partners learn more about what is ailing the relationship and troubling each of them if we refuse to referee their fights.

Luckily, most couples get quiet long enough for us to introduce the idea that their success in therapy would be largely determined by their willingness to work toward each of them taking responsibility for their own personal happiness.

Once they are seated in their respective corners of the ring, we can guide them toward an understanding of the way they each participate in the blame game, and its effect on their romantic health. If we are not lured into taking sides it is easier for us to introduce them to the notion that they are each responsible for everything they think, feel and do. Granted this is not true for minors or adults who are mentally or physically dependent on others. But all mentally competent, physically capable adults are responsible for their own feelings and actions. It's not always a popular position, and we hold it to be absolutely true.

It is important to understand, we are not suggesting you are responsible for how hurtful people behave toward you. We are asking you to consider that you are responsible for the way you

Self-care – The Third Building Block

continue to feel for the wrongs you suffered in the past. And if you are going to be free of the chains of resentment and reclaim your life, you will need to understand something about who hurt you.

Little is known about why humans hurt other humans, however, we know for sure that hurt people turn around and hurt other people if they do not resolve the injuries they first endured. Developing a clearer understanding of the purpose of someone's behavior can be of enormous value in understanding the wrong they have committed and placing it into a clear perspective. That is not to say we support the habit of making excuses for other people's mistreatment of us. The relief that you would gain from such a strategy would be fleeting. Nor are we asking you to create justifications for someone else's hurtful behavior. The challenge here is to understand that, in some cases, the wrongdoer was living life according to a pattern, or a reaction, that had nothing to do with you. You, through perhaps no fault of your own, were in the wrong place at the right time.

Consider this example:

Harry is walking through a patient wing of the local hospital to visit an elderly relative recovering from a recent fall. As he passes an open doorway to a patient room, he notices Bob, a dear friend from high school, lying in the bed staring out the window. He decides to be friendly, as he once had a great relationship with Bob and this is a perfect opportunity to reconnect. He decides to pay him a quick visit with the hopes of rekindling the bond they shared from the old days.

Harry enters the room to see if he could seize the moment to reclaim a lost friendship and is greeted with an angry outburst from Bob who screams obscenities and chastises Harry for entering where he was not welcome. Harry leaves quickly to avoid further attacks and wanders down the hallway somewhat dazed by the rude and ungrateful reception he has received by Bob. He realizes that they had not had contact for over 20 years but he thinks he deserved better than that. "The hell with Bob," he thinks. "He has become a real snob since hitting it big in the stock market" and "he was obviously not a real friend anyway".

Along the way to his relative's room, Harry runs into Sam, another member of his graduating class that he sees on occasion, and proceeds to assassinate Bob's character for how he was treated by him. Harry is good and mad and certain that his anger is justified. "I had a good mind to go back there and knock him off of his high horse". He will never speak to Bob again and regrets ever thinking that they could be friends again. He had done without Bob for 20 years and could continue on without him just fine.

Sam knows better than to interrupt Harry in his vengeful counterattack on Bob, because Harry believes himself to be the victim of a personal attack and he knows Harry has always positioned himself in the role of the victim of other people's hurtful behavior. When Harry has exhausted the emotional fuel he was burning, Sam suggests that Harry might have it all wrong. He explains that Bob and his family had been in a car accident that morning and that Bob was the only survivor. His wife and two children had died on the way to the hospital.

The anger quickly drains out of Harry's face as he listens to the tragic account of the accident. Bob had not launched a personal attack on Harry. Bob just launched an attack and Harry was available.

People from all walks of life seem to develop, without any direct instruction, a core belief that other people, places and circumstances or events are responsible for the way they may feel on a given day. The idea that there must be someone to blame for times of chaos or discontent seems to have been our birthright. The need to find a scapegoat to blame for the quality of life seems to have always been with our species. Many people will defend their right to brand someone or something for what is wrong as if it were a liberty, like freedom of speech or the right to vote. We cannot be sure if other animals blame each other when things do not go well in their environment, but the tendency for humans to blame other humans appears to be as old as recorded history.

People sue other people every day because a defendant has hurt their feelings. Some people change romantic partners as frequently as they do their underwear and not necessarily with much more thought. Romantic partners end relationships every day because one or both partners subscribe to the belief that the other partner is the cause of the pain in their lives and that they will be "better off" without him or her.

Maybe you have thought about ending a romance because you caught sight of the greener romantic "grass" on the other side of the fence. Or, maybe you simply concluded that all would be well if you rid yourself of your romantic partner. Either way, the act of blaming others for the way you feel hardly ever leads to a meaningful solution. The only strategy more likely to ensure romantic failure and promote widespread unhappiness is running from problems.

On your mark, get set ...

Prior to our marriage the two of us ended many romantic relationships with no more thought then "it seemed like a good thing to do at the time." We managed to become quite adept at running from romantic commitments. If there were Olympic medals for world-class achievement in the area of romantic sabotage, we would have placed honorably in the ranking. However, our real accomplishments would have been in events that showcased skills associated with the avoidance of problems and eluding commitments. In particular, John would have surely found his way onto the cover of a cereal box with a lucrative endorsement contract for one of his grandest runs ever had he not gotten blocked by a wall at the finish line.

In the early days of his recovery from alcoholism and drug addiction, John struggled to face the challenges of life without some type of anesthetic to take the edge off. He had managed to get and stay sober through the fellowship of a self-help group. Unfortunately he had not addressed all of his "drugs of choice." As he always had, he took comfort in the pursuit of one romantic relationship after another.

Most of the first three years of his sobriety were spent chasing one romantic interest after another without awareness of, or regard for, the harms he was causing himself and others. He was someone whose worst day sober was *not* better than his best day drinking, as most others in recovery culture would say. His unbridled love and sex addiction hurled him wildly out of control through the hearts and lives of others. He cheated on every romantic partner and could only manage to hold on to long-term relationships if they lived a long distance from him. While he was somewhat aware that he had a problem with women, he was pretty sure that his romantic failures were the result of having made poor choices. He joked with friends about having a "broken picker" but the partners from whom he ran never got the joke.

In his eyes, something was always wrong with his romantic partners. It was never his fault. He had just never found the right person. At least that was the story he frequently promoted until his infamous run into the priesthood.

He attended a major university, which unfortunately supported the belief of the times that homosexuality was a pathological condition warranting treatment. Sitting in a lecture one day, John paid little attention to the guest lecturer, until he began outlining the signs of latent homosexuality. The "expert" told the class that latent homosexuals were "incapable of maintaining a sustained and monogamous relationship with a member of the opposite sex" and would "never be free until they claimed the truth about themselves." John hurried from the lecture hall as soon as the class was dismissed, and pondered the indictment he had just received. This was it. He finally had an answer to why he could not maintain a romantic commitment. He was unknowingly homosexual.

It was the newest excuse or explanation for what was wrong with him. He reflected briefly on the fact he had never had a romantic or sexual attraction toward other men, or any same-sex sexual contact, but did not give it much thought. That is not a surprise. Self-examination was not a strong suit of his. He was all about blaming someone for his problems, running from them, or both. Now, he told himself, he had found the explanation for why he could not stay committed in a romance, and why he mistrusted and objectified women.

And from that, followed the solution. John would become a priest. This, he thought, would surely put an end to his reign of romantic terror and provide him with a sanctuary from all the trouble he was in. He enlisted a family member to arrange for him to meet a "priest recruiter," as he referred to him. At the time, he happened to be on the run from the consequences of his love and sex addiction, and was looking for a reason to break off a romance empty of intrigue or excitement. The priesthood would also be a great place to hide, re-gain him status with his family, and gain him respect in the community.

During the weeks leading up to his interview, he put on such an evangelical performance that he came to believe his own "press releases". He stopped cursing and gossiping about others, went to Mass daily and was usually seen with a bible under his arm. Many applauded his decision, but his closest friends dismissed it as an elaborate scheme to get out of a romantic commitment he was never going to honor.

His grandmother, who always saw the good in him, cheerfully welcomed his offer to bless her bingo cards. Because he was going to commit himself to a life of poverty, she gave him money whenever she saw him. He spent weeks clearing out all relationships because they stood in the way of his commitment to God. At least, this is what he told himself when he broke up with his romantic partner. She painfully accepted his claim that the breakup was for her own good because God had revealed they were not meant for each other. He never told her that he was going to become a priest. No surprise there. She would not have bought it anymore than his friends had.

On the scheduled day, he took off for his appointment with Father Joe, convinced that God had called him to the religious vocation and the recruiter would want to enlist him immediately. The interview lasted about thirty minutes. All but the last few minutes went by in a flash. He quickly and confidently told the good Father of his desire to join the priesthood and of his belief that his "calling" was the most authentic and moving experience he'd ever had next to drinking grain alcohol. Father Joe seemed most attentive. His warm reception confirmed for John that he would surely be fast-tracked to the holy vocation.

When he finished, the old priest cleared his throat, folded him arms across his chest and gave a warm note of gratitude,

"My son, I am so glad you came today for the priesthood truly needs good young men; however, you appear to be running from something."

John didn't register what came after the objection, other than the vague sense that Father Joe tried to help him get to the bottom of what was troubling him. Other than hearing the word "running" it was all a blur. The rejection did not hit him until the drive back to his college dorm. While flirting with coeds in halter tops, he cursed the priest for having blocked his attempt to follow the path that he was certain God had laid out for him. He returned to his co-ed dorm and found a female bandage for his wound.

John was a mess for several weeks. You see, Father Joe's warning, which he remembered the following morning, reverberated in him every time his thoughts were not occupied. The priest had closed the interview with the hope that John would "stay where he was at until leaving was not the solution to the problem." John had missed out on many opportunities to truly examine himself. He was always running from a problem to a solution without ever understanding what was wrong with him.

You might think the wall he hit with Father Joe's rejection would have been enough to get his attention. Sadly his self-delusion continued for another three months during which time he assassinated Father Joe's character. After the three months, he found himself truly alone and still unhappy. He had cut his ties with anyone who had wanted to be close to him, and had no one to blame for things.

Finally, he was encouraged into a process of self-examination by a friend and he surprisingly, accepted. For John, it was a rare period of introspection. During the process, he remembered a time as a child, when he overheard two men gossiping about his father, blaming him for something that had gone wrong. The men commented that

Self-care – The Third Building Block

John's dad had never lost an argument but had certainly managed to lose quite a few friends.

John had gone to sleep many a night while his parents battled in the kitchen below his bedroom. He had promised God he would never be like his dad, who was a drunk, mean-spirited and always hurting someone. This prayerful promise had often been his only comfort. As he reflected on this, it was revealed to him that the prayerful promise ended up more like a self-fulfilling prophecy. He had been trying to avoid becoming his dad. In the process, he learned to blame him for everything that was wrong in his life, from being a fat kid to having a bad temper. Fully established by the time John was six years of age, the blame game had allowed him to hold others responsible for his poor choices, unkind and manipulative behavior, and to maintain a blind eye to his own wrongs.

This realization was part of the emotional awakening he underwent.

Many times, we can become obsessed with resentment over the wrongs we have had to endure. We often wrongly assume there must be something inherently wrong with us, or people would not have treated us so poorly. The harms others caused us had little or nothing to do with who we were, or how we behaved. Others were troubled, and we became their victims. This is an important point to reflect upon. Many of us have spent years believing we were flawed because of the way others treated us. We decided our supposed brokenness somehow caused others to disregard or neglect our needs, or behave abusively. Injury can surely cause flaws, but we were not injured because we were flawed. The two of us have come to understand after a great deal of self-examination of our resentments that our perceptions were flawed, not our personhood.

John's father frequently shamed him with the admonition that if he "lived to be one hundred years old he would never become the man" his father had. He had spent years trying to prove his father wrong. Unfortunately, he employed many of his father's strategies for coping with other people. Now he shuttered to think he had become more like his dad than he had ever feared. Both he and his father were never wrong about anything and always found someone to blame for what was wrong in their lives. The awareness left him certain he needed to stop the blame game. He alone was responsible for the quality of his own life. He had made up his mind to change.

The only way to change is to change

So, what was next? If you have been absorbing our material thus far, you should be able to guess. We must change.

> Before we summarize the two simple ingredients critical to changing your romantic health, it is time for a pop quiz:
>
> ~
>
> There were three frogs sitting on a log.
>
> One frog decided to jump into the pond.
>
> How many were left?
>
> ~

If you know more about human behavior than you do math, you would have guessed right. Three frogs were still on the log because nothing actually happened. Making a decision to jump is not an action; it is a thought. Change requires more than thoughts, insights and decisions. And, we have to change in two ways critical to romantic health.

First, you must surrender your "right" to blame your romantic partner for any of your thoughts, feelings and actions.

Second, you have to "stay where you are at" until leaving is no longer the solution to any of the problems you are experiencing in the relationship. In other words, no running.

The first action of change is to acknowledge that you are responsible for the quality of your own life. We know that it may sound a little hokey but try saying it out loud to yourself. "I am responsible for the way I think and feel and for all of my actions".

Self-care – The Third Building Block

How did you feel when you said it? The first time either one of us considered this radical position we were immediately flooded by a barrage of dissenting thoughts. It was as if the words were streaming from the haunted recesses of our innermost selves. Initially the voices in our head said:

> "Really? Are you kidding? The people who beat and abused you are responsible for who you have become. You are damaged goods. It is not your fault but you are stuck with the personality that your past created!"

Unfortunately this was not a one-time appearance from the haunting committee. The objections continued for several months and usually ended with something like:

> "Besides, why would you want to let them off them off the hook for ruining your life?"

The phantom voices were attempting to convince us that other people, places and events were responsible for the problems in our lives, that we were entitled to the resentments we harbored. They were our rewards for the suffering we had endured. As you know from our stories, when we collapsed in emotional bankruptcy we possessed very little except the resentments that we had clung to for years.

In our journey to health we learned a funny thing about resentments. We thought that we were getting even with all the people who had harmed us by hating and blaming them for our lack of success — we were wrong. You see, resentments are actually the poisons we intend for the people who had hurt us, but that we end up drinking. We were further disheartened to discover that we had done more harm to ourselves with our faulty thinking and actions than any of the villains or hazardous situations in our lives.

We were going about life all wrong. It became painfully clear. All positive change occurs from the inside out and is not dependent on the attitudes and actions of others. We had wasted years trying to change people, places and circumstances and all we had to show for it was a long list of resentments.

We abandoned the idea that other people were responsible for the quality of our lives and extinguished the flames of resentment that held our happiness in the hands of others. But we had one more preliminary action to take when we realized that running away from problems was a race that we could never win. We had run from challenges, discomfort, love, affection and responsibility. You see, it did not matter whether what we feared might hurt us or be good for us – we ran. The following prayer provided the spiritual motivation we needed for hanging up our running shoes:

> God, grant me the serenity
> to accept the things I cannot change,
> The courage to change the things I can,
> And wisdom to know the difference.
> Reinhold Niebuhr

If religious references like God do not work for you that is okay. You can derive considerable benefit from the Serenity Prayer by viewing the letters god as an acronym for Good Orderly Direction.

We knew the decision to give up running without purposeful action would mean little. The action we took to symbolize hanging up our running shoes – since we were not actually runners – was an LOL we call "Tearing up the IOUs."

Tearing up your IOUs

Few habits will impair the progress that you and your partner can achieve toward creating romantic health than the habit of maintaining resentments. The resentments that you and your partner may be holding on to for each other should have been addressed prior to completing your Joint Safety Plan. If other resentments have surfaced

Self-care – The Third Building Block

in your memory or occurred since then, please address them before moving on. We do not want that baggage weighing you down.

The IOUs that we are targeting in this LOL are related to institutions and people who have wronged you other than your romantic partner. You may not be able to address them all the first time around because the most enduring resentments may seem to have become a part of your view of life. Be patient with yourself and prepare to tear up as many as you can and hold onto those that will require more work until you have learned to live without resentment.

On the next page you will be provided with an example of a completed IOU Coupon for you to use as a reference.

LOL
Tearing Up Your IOUs

We have provided you with a really cute little IOU Coupon for you to replicate and use in this LOL. Alongside the heading of "Perpetrator" you are to write the name of the person, institution or group that you resent. Remember, you do not need proof of the wrong or the identity of person or group responsible. Second, alongside the title "Nature of Burden" briefly describe the consequence with which they left you burdened with. You are free to describe what your perpetrators did to you, but for this action of change it is not necessary. The important thing is that you describe the burden they left you. Alongside the last title, "Cost of the IOU", write something about what each of the IOU's have cost you. You will create an additional IOU for each person, organization or group that you have held resentments for.

Once you have finished all your coupons, share your work with your partner and consider tearing up the IOU's as a symbol of your willingness to drop the resentment and move on. Remember that consideration of an action is only a thought. If you are ready to move on, then tear up your IOU's and throw them away.

I.O.U. Coupon

Perpetrator: Father

Nature of the Burden: Left me with low self-esteem

Cost of the IOU:

Many people have tried to validate my needs and interests but I dismissed them because the attempts were not coming from my father.

Ready to care

You have now undertaken two actions of change. The first was taking personal responsibility for the quality of your own life. It may have seemed quite simple but, as you have probably guessed, it will require considerable ongoing effort. The second action of tearing up your IOU's may have required great effort and sacrifice but you are not actually forfeiting anything of value. It is not as if you can cash them in for a vacation cruise or a toaster oven. These two simple actions can go a long way in promoting the opportunity for meaningful change. Now let us move on to your initial self-care plans.

My self-care plan

The self-care plans you and your partner create should be crafted in a way that ensures your goals are achievable and are not so exhaustive as to leave either of you unable to respond to the ever changing demands of a full and productive life.

There is no "one-size-fits-all" self-care plan. Each of us has to develop our own plan because each of us has our own unique life story, limitations, strengths, challenges and we each have individual goals and dreams.

The process of creating a self-care plan can become quite involved especially if it is intended to be comprehensive. The level of detail you build into your plan is entirely up to you. We encourage you to begin with a simple self-care plan. The format we introduce is intended to focus your attention on those actions that will enhance the quality of your romantic relationship. The initial plan is intended to support your work as a couple for the first thirty days but can be altered at any time as needed.

We would suggest you begin with one care objective for each of the areas that you experience in life. In so doing you will examine your physical, emotional, spiritual and work/leisure (play) domains with an eye for how you are going to reduce stressors and/or enhance the quality of your romantic relationship. The initial plan we suggest involves identifying one observable behavior you can introduce or eliminate in each of the four domains. Please select action choices that represent a change to how you are currently living. In addition to providing a label for each behavior, add a brief explanation for why you have chosen it.

On the following page we offer a sample of a completed Self-care Plan to illustrate how this LOL can be used.

Optimally, you and your partner's self-care plans will be better developed than this illustration. We intend it to be a starting point. Remember, as we have discussed earlier, both you and your partner need to be open to input from each other about action steps that might be critical to the safety and overall health of the relationship.

If you are developing a comprehensive self-care plan, include goals and objectives you have already implemented as well as those you believe should be added. This model is not designed to look at assets and liabilities, only at areas of needed change as they relate to your romance.

If you and your partner have reviewed and approved each other's self-care plans, it is time to move to the fourth and final building block. So, let's get to work on completing your self-care plans so you can share them with each other and look for ways to support each other's success.

LOL
My Self-care Plan

You will note in the completed Self-care Plan below that there is an observable behavior that is being introduced or eliminated in each of the four areas. There is a brief explanation for why the change of behavior was chosen below each identified behavior.

Physical

Reduce caffeine intake by 50%

Caffeine makes me really irritable and much less able to remain engaged with you in conversations as a result.

Emotional

Journal on a daily basis to log exposure to stressors that I can share with my partner.

I have so much stress at work that I don't like to talk about it so instead I block it out before I get home but I guess my misery hurts our relationship and I should talk about what is bothering me.

Spiritual

Read inspirational material dealing with positive thinking on a daily basis for 30 minutes and share any insights gained with my partner.

I have so many sources of negativity in my life that it is difficult to feel optimistic. I could use help from reading positive sources of inspiration.

Work/Play

Update my resume so I will have an increased opportunity to pursue other employment options.

I have done nothing for the past two years about the hostile work environment. I need to start the process of looking for relief. I feel so drained from work that there is no time to enjoy my partner or my life.

7

Emotional Bonding
The Fourth Building Block

The notion of being responsible to and not responsible for a loved one can be difficult to swallow for many people, but the concept has been around for thousands of years in a variety of forms

• • • • • • • • • • • • • • • • •

    A commitment to be *IN* Love requires each partner to invest time and emotional energy into the development and maintenance of an emotional bond. Emotional Bonding is a feeling and interactive process. It both relies on, and generates trust and affection. A bond of this type develops when humans face extreme stress together, such as combat or a fatal illness. Relax! We are not promoting that you and your partner pursue either path. Instead we are encouraging the type of bonding that occurs when two people are responsible to each other.

Responsible To...

No, we are not asking you to be responsible for each other. In fact, we discourage such a practice because it generally causes a great many problems too complicated for us to explore in this book. We are asking you to be responsible *to* – not *for* – your partner. The difference is a fundamental one and easy to misconstrue. We are encouraging you to *give* care to – not *take* care of – someone.

Mary Jane and Robert

Robert came to us some years ago claiming that his wife's over-spending was ruining their marriage and his career, as well as destroying the quality of his life. He spoke in great detail about his failed attempts at getting Mary Jane to control her over-spending. Many sleepless nights were spent ruminating over the impotence he felt when trying to change her behavior in order to improve things for himself. He was depressed and felt he was failing his wife and his children for being powerless over whether or not Mary Jane blew the budget on a given day. His career as a military officer had put him in the position of directing the lives of tens of thousands of troops with great success. He could not believe that he was unable to bring his wife's spending problem, and therefore his home, under control.

Before Robert could be trained to conduct an intervention for Mary Jane, he needed to spend many hours working with us to reclaim responsibility for the quality of his own life. After several months of preparation the intervention team was successful in motivating Mary Jane to get the help that she needed. It was difficult at first for any of the friends and family on the intervention team to understand the difference between being responsible to Mary Jane versus responsible for her. Because of the work he had done on himself, Robert was able to help them over the hurdles he had successfully cleared.

Initially Robert fought the idea of allowing Mary Jane to be responsible for the emotional consequences her behavior was causing. He believed it would be a betrayal of his wedding vows. With time, Robert came to see that loving Mary Jane meant bringing his concerns directly to her in a loving way. That way, she could experience the emotional discomfort needed to create a desire to change. He came to understand that loving anyone first meant taking responsibility for the quality of his own life. Part of taking responsibility meant learning to bring his concerns, insights, experience, strength, and hope to those he cared about. He has long since learned to be a care*giver* rather than a care*taker*.

The notion of being responsible to and not responsible for a loved one can be difficult to swallow for many people, but the concept has been around for thousands of years in a variety of forms. Being responsible to someone can be likened to the act of being of service to them whereas being responsible for someone suggests we should be in control of them. Many folks are fearful of acting controlling with those they love. You don't have to worry. First, you can't be controlling when you are being of service. Second, you NEVER have CONTROL over others anyway.

In our daily mediation book for couples, *One in the Spirit: A Meditation Course for Recovering Couples©*, we address the challenges that go with being of service to our romantic partners.

The following is an excerpt:

Challenge

Many of us struggle with what to do when a loved one is troubled in some way. Some of us believe that we need to mind our own business: it is not my place to say anything! Others interpret detachment as a license to disregard the responsibility for loving another person. Still others would rush into every problem to "fix it", regardless of whether or not they have permission.

The meditation course meets every challenge that couples face with a Reflection that is intended to help the partners to meet the particular challenge with practical tools. The Reflection that follows the above Challenge offers:

Reflection

While it is true that you cannot control the physical, emotional, and spiritual health of your mate, you share a responsibility for being of service to them when you are spiritually fit. Few people will be as well equipped as you are to see the signs that your mate is struggling, but personal interest can hinder the very best insight. If your words are selfish or hurtful, you are only hindering progress. If you want to be helpful, you must first look inside yourself. What is your personal identification with the problem and how might your life experiences be affecting how you are sharing your concern? Is your concern for your partner's struggle made worse by your fear of how it will affect your security? The struggles of our partner greatly influence us and if it is not our business, then whose business is it?

Emotional Bonding – The Fourth Building Block

Another excerpt from the book that might encourage you to consider the therapeutic value of being responsible to your partner is found in a reflection on the *Challenge of Detachment vs. Responsibility*, a title of one of our meditations in the same book, which encourages romantic partners to learn to be of service rather than attempting to remain in love while detaching.

The following is an excerpt:

Challenge

Learning how to detach from the problems and mood swings of a partner is a difficult task for many of us. Detachment is understood to involve a "disconnection" from the lives of our mates when they are troubled. How do I serve my partner in a way that shows my love for them rather than my responsibility for them?

Reflection

It is easy to say that the emotional and spiritual well-being of your partner is not your problem. However, such a position of complete separation will rob your partner of needed love, support, and insight. Instead of totally disconnecting, you may be able to help at one of these crucial times with gentle and rigorous honesty. This does not suggest that it is acceptable for your partner to blame you for the qualities of his/her life or that you are responsible for making it better. We are encouraging your involvement in the solution, not asking you to fix the problem. You can be helpful by sharing your concerns, experience, strength, and hope without trying to control the outcome. A healthy balance can be obtained that lies somewhere in between being totally disconnected and being the "fixer." Because we have found that we are either a part of the problem or a part of the solution in relationships, we have learned to be responsible first to our Higher Power and then to each other. Do not post the blame. Do not accept the blame. Moreover, do not ignore your responsibility.

Detachment is not a break of contact or a separation.

We are sure that some, perhaps much of this thinking, will run contrary to many things you were taught about romantic love. We are not asking you to abandon your old ideas completely and buy into our philosophy. Put your old rules for romantic engagement on the back burner for 90 days and try something different.

It may take some time for the two of you to learn a different way of responding to each other's emotional states and behavior that you find objectionable in the other, but you can get there. If we were able to do it with all of our dysfunctional cultural heritage and emotional baggage then YOU CAN DO IT. You will need practice and a commitment to remain connected to each other. If you are thinking right now that "this is a great deal of work with no real guarantee", perhaps you might not even be sure of wanting this level of intimacy. If so, we encourage you to take an honest look at your hopes and dreams. We are not suggesting that you gaze into the rearview mirror to remind yourself of what you and your partner once shared. There will be time for that. For now we want you to focus your attention on the romantic standards you have for the young people in your life.

Romantic hopes & dreams

When we were first considering a very different approach to romance, we did not know what to hope for. The only history we could reference came from our caregivers, and we knew we did not want to follow their examples. We also knew we still loved each other, but the bonding and close attachment that used to come without effort was beginning to require work.

We weren't afraid of working hard. The problem for us was one of direction — we had none. One of us, (it was so long ago we can no longer remember who) thought of looking at the dreams we had for our children, who at that time were in elementary school. We found that, when we focused on what we wanted their romantic lives to look like, we received the inspiration we needed. We were able to work on new tools for our romantic maintenance.

Emotional Bonding – The Fourth Building Block

Once again, romantic health requires considerable effort and real action. Do not give into the widely held belief that romantic love is reserved for the young. That is the road most often traveled. We are proposing a road less traveled

Please do not be discouraged. If you have read this far it is a pretty good guess you are not ready to give up on your romance or the idea of being *IN* Lov*e*. Good for you. If you found yourself reading our story and thinking "We're not nearly as bad as those two and if they can make it so can we," good for you. You are right. If you are questioning your resolve because John and Elaine are both seasoned therapists and you are sure you won't be able to behave like therapists with each other, good for you. No, really!

It is fortunate for you that you will not have the extra burden of repeatedly stopping each other from playing therapist in the relationship. It is to your advantage. Therapists can behave like hopeless romantics and unyielding critics all in the same argument. We have had our share of arguments where we both found ourselves held hostage to believing we were somewhat at fault, yet certain the other person was more to blame.

We have no desire to tell you what your romance should look like or what being in love should feel like. We believe you and your partner already have a pretty good idea of both, and how you choose to define them is entirely up to you. You need to be the ones to decide what you want. We do have a desire that you not settle for less than the romance you want for yourselves, your children and other loved ones.

Let us stop for a moment and examine the type of romance you really want by developing a one-sided conversation with your child or loved one. This suggestion might make you ask, "What do our dreams for the happiness of our children or loved ones have to do with the struggles we are having in our romance?" We are inviting you to look at the desires you have for them. Your dreams for their romantic happiness can provide you with a peek into your innermost desires for your own, no matter how far down you have tried to stuff them.

If exciting and passionate love is possible for your grandchildren, it is possible for you. If you have a desire for your son to know true partnership with his mate, then you know it is what you want in your own life.

So please allow yourself to do some dreaming by completing the following LOL, titled *Letter of Romantic Hope & Dreams*, to your child or grandchild. If you don't have a child or loved one to write to, do not fret. All of us will tap into our inner being and identify our own desire and needs if we trick ourselves into thinking about what we would want for an innocent loved one like a grandchild.

When you have completed the LOL letter, do not share it with the person to whom you have written it, unless they are age appropriate and you have their consent to do so.

After completing the writing, please re-read what you have written out loud to yourself and allow yourself to experience the feelings that flow from your reflections on all that you have written.

We encourage you to share your Letter of Romantic Hopes & Dreams with your romantic partner. If your experience of sharing it is rewarding, please take a day or two to enjoy each other's company before exploring the tool kit that we have prepared for you in the following chapter. Please keep in mind that you are building the foundation with your movement through this book. The exercises are not intended to be a rush or crash course.

In the following chapter we will introduce you to additional tools you and your partner can use to building Emotional Bonding.

Emotional Bonding – The Fourth Building Block

LOL
Letter of Romantic Hopes & Dreams

Make every effort to communicate the thoughts and feelings you have as you reflect on the questions. Do not limit yourself to the space provided. Write your answers or reflections on a separate sheet of paper. Remember, you are creating a type of love letter to your loved one (child or grandchild) so write it from your heart.

What do you imagine or believe that your loved one will have to offer to a romantic relationship that would be of value to a partner who is looking for a life-long commitment?

Describe how you would like your loved one to feel when his or her partner enters the room.

Identify some of the challenges that your loved one will face during the life of his or her romance and how you would hope that he or she will respond to them.

What would you tell your loved one to do when he or she feels hurt in the romance and wants to run to the imagined relief of a breakup or the seduction of another romantic interest?

Describe how you felt about yourself and your partner when your current relationship began and what you believed would come of your dreams together.

Describe what you would be willing to do to return to the hopeful moments when your relationship began.

Close off your letter to your loved one with your hope for what being "in love" will look like and feel like for him or her.

8

Tools for Emotional Bonding

Romantic relationships become sanctuaries when they are places of mutual support and intimate positive regard

• • • • • • • • • • • • • • • • •

There are many ways for romantic partners to restore or enhance their emotional bond. If you are thinking, "Heh, they are suggesting that we take an active role in supporting each other's personal growth efforts", you are close. We are actually asking you and your partner to assume therapeutic responsibilities in each other's lives.

Some of our clients challenge our recommendation to actively participate in their partner's self-care plan. They object, "We are not therapists ... we don't know how to be therapeutic with our partner" Our response is pretty simple and straightforward. You will either learn to be therapeutic in the relationship or you will be countertherapeutic — the choice is yours.

We have found four tools to be particularly reliable and they are: Mutual Support, Shared Accountability, Reciprocal *IN*put and Daily Connection.

They will aid you and your partner to develop an emotional bond every bit as magical as it was when the two of you seemed inseparable.

Mutual Support

The first tool for promoting Emotional Bonding is Mutual Support. The idea of deriving support from a romantic partnership is hardly a novel idea. Most married couples we see made some kind of vow or commitment to Mutual Support on their wedding day that they were expected to uphold until death. Actually, these definitive declarations usually begin during the courtship. In fact, during the opening chapters of most romantic relationships the partners enthusiastically look for opportunities to be of service to each other. They quickly come to rely on each other for support of all kinds, often to the exclusion of pre-existing friendships and life-long family relationships.

Humans appear to be hardwired for Mutual Support – to seek out connection with others and to work cooperatively. Unfortunately, a desire to be close and supportive is quite different from a demonstrated willingness to do whatever it takes to achieve it. In the early months of a romance it is fairly easy to maintain an emotional connection but over time it tends to fade, or when not nurtured, to fail.

Support takes time

Many couples understand that romance requires effort, but find it difficult to make time for it given the demands of raising a family. This is especially true now that, financially, most families need both partners to work. We understand there are only so many free hours in a day. It's important to remember the well known wisdom of commercial flight attendants, secure the oxygen masks on yourself before helping your children or others. You and your partner must put your need for mutual emotional support ahead of the endless stream of little league games, scouting events, bake sales, family vacations, and the other flood of demands for our time.

Tools for Emotional Bonding

While raising our own children, we attended graduate school, managed our careers and honored our commitments to be of service to others. At times it was very difficult to find the time to invest in our romance. We tried unsuccessfully to make up for it with "quality time," whatever that means. The eloquent dinners and date night retreats were great while they lasted. Their benefits were usually pretty short-lived. Eventually we realized that quality time cannot take the place of a commitment to fully support each other's emotional and spiritual health.

The romance industry spends a great deal of their marketing dollars promoting quality time with everything from greeting cards to romantic getaways. It is a quick fix, and quick fixes do not create sustained bonds. Most of us cannot even remember how we felt on vacation a month after returning to the office. We are encouraging you to make an investment in your relationship. It is unlikely you and your partner can thrive as a couple all week long because you had a really great date-night on Saturday, or a satisfying sexual encounter while playing hooky from work and responsibilities.

Mutual Support requires time and commitment. This is especially true if your romance is healing from a betrayal, financial hardship, chronic illness or other such threats. It can also be a great deal more challenging if either or both of you grew up in a family racked by addiction or mental illness. The skills for maintaining emotional attachment may have been difficult to acquire and therefore a struggle to draw from. Romantic partners who were raised in such environments need a good deal of both quantity and quality time to maintain romantic health.

Got hugs?

Regular purposeful connection at physical, emotional and spiritual levels with your partner is vital. You are not likely to enjoy sustained success in your attempts to be *IN* Love if you do not work every day at being connected.

Virginia Satir, a psychotherapist and author often regarded as the mother of family therapy, prescribed the following:

> We need 4 hugs a day for survival.
> We need 8 hugs a day for maintenance.
> We need 12 hugs a day for growth.
> – Virginia Satir

We suspect she would agree that quality cannot replace quantity. In the coming pages we provide you with several tools for making a connection with your partner, thereby promoting Emotional Bonding. For the time being, why not take Satir's prescription?

- Hug your partner at least 12 times a day
- Have each hug last at least one minute
- Avoid the urge to talk during the hug
- Do not pat each other on the back during the time lapse — just hug
- While you hold onto each other, shift your focus between hugging and being hugged

When the minute is up, let your partner know what you received from the experience is just a few words. These verbal investments help you to feel safe with your partner, thereby supporting your efforts to implement the tools of Shared Accountability explained below.

Shared Accountability

The tool of Shared Accountability, while listed second, is a critical resource for couples looking to promote increased Emotional Bonding. The use of accountability partners has found a place in every aspect of our culture from Fortune 500 companies to weight-loss franchises and religious congregations. The monitoring provided by accountability partners promotes support between partners to achieve goals associated with business or fitness plans, promote adherence to moral values and abstinence from addictive disorders, to name just a few. The role of an accountability partner varies with the goal that has been targeted for the organization supporting the benefits of having an accountability partner.

You and your partner can form Shared Accountability for each other's physical, emotional and spiritual well-being. Few people have more access to either of you than you do to each other. Generally, you have front row seats for witnessing events that our friends and family only hear about, sometimes well after the fact. Unfortunately, as time goes by, our romantic partners can become the very last people to whom we reach out, if we have not cut them off completely.

Like some of our clients, you might believe it is naturally easier to confide in a friend, family member or co-worker than in your partner because they speak to you without resentment. It may very well be easier, however, not naturally so. More likely it is easier because they speak to you without resentment and bitterness stemming from hurtful behavior on your part.

We always hurt the ones we love

It is a great song title. It's also a painfully sad commentary on the tendency for us to hurt the people we claim to love. This is especially true with our romantic partners. We are most likely to show our true colors when we are with our partners and usually will not pretend that we are ok when we are not. Sadly, the same people who get to see the "real me" are the ones we tend to shy away from when we need support, inspiration or help to see our blind spots.

The people we are most intimate with can be the biggest targets for our foul moods and unkind behavior. We think that is because they are often the most revealing mirrors in our lives. By mirrors we mean that we are oftentimes able to see what is wrong with ourselves when we are in their presence. It is as if they reflect what is wrong with us that others cannot see. They are frequently dumped on, avoided or blamed for what is wrong with our lives. They represent mirrors that have to be broken or pushed away when we do not what to look too closely at ourselves. We have unfortunately suffered through many such periods or episodes in our life together.

John remembers one such period, which he and Elaine hope they never forget, which began when their first child was only six weeks old. As new parents, we were thrilled to have such a trouble free child who frequently slept through the night the first day out of the hospital and generally filled up quick during feedings. The blessing we imagined it to be was quickly diminished at the conclusion of his six-week check up. His pediatrician struggled to maintain eye contact as he broke the news that Shawn's innocent heart murmur was probably much more serious. And so it was. We were flooded with fear for the year prior to his open-heart surgery, which he might survive long enough to risk the 50-50 chance of recovering from.

Those awful months before the surgery created greater torment than I had suffered as a child. No matter what I did, I could not manage to regain the hope and sense of purpose I had come to enjoy in life. I was afraid, angry and unapproachable from the moment we first learned of Shawn's congenital heart defect to the moment we kissed him goodbye and watched him wheeled into surgery.

Neither Elaine nor I could find much relief from the fear but that was not the greatest anguish I endured. I had resolved myself to believe that Shawn was going to die no matter what was done. In the loneliness before each morning dawn I often wished God would take my son, so that his mom and I, and most likely him, could stop the suffering. The wish would trigger blinding terror and send me racing into Shawn's nursery to make sure he was still breathing. Just before dawn I would fall asleep during guard duty with my hand resting on his chest, in case his heart stopped. They were the darkest moments of my life.

There would be many such moments during the year before Shawn's surgery when I seemed incapable of sharing with even my closest friends. That was not the worst of it. I kept everyone at bay, especially Elaine – the one person who could know what I was really feeling and might be able to help me. She and I grew further and further apart because I ran from her. I imagined that Elaine could see through the smoke screen I had created for everyone else. If we got too close, I would not be able to hide from the fear and anger that haunted me. I could see my emotions reflected back to me in her blood shot eyes and worn expression. I did whatever was needed to do to break the mirror she represented. Within one year, our emotional bond deteriorated to the point where we only talk about our son's heart disease.

Finding a great accountability partner

Our romantic partners get us at our best and our worse. If we cannot turn to them as confidantes and sources of support, then we are likely to push them away when we are not doing well as we have described above. We understand that it can be really challenging to take a hard look at ourselves but we must face the difficult truth and get help, or break the mirrors in our lives.

Patterns of hurting those we love can be interrupted and changed, and the relationship can become a source of mutual strength, if we are willing to look into the mirror and change. The two of us took that vital step when we became each other's accountability partners.

Mutual Check-IN

A Mutual Check-*IN* is one of our favorite LOLs for couples committed to being *IN* Love, and looking for ways to be accountability partners. The partners can meet on a weekly, monthly or as needed basis to review the challenges and victories that each has encountered in their individual journey in life.

The frequency of Check-*IN*s should be determined by the level of stability in the relationship and the level of challenge that either you or your partner are facing. Efforts should be made to keep the meetings under one hour if you are scheduling them regularly. You may find it necessary to meet for longer periods from time to time, but if long meetings are the norm, you will probably abandon the tool.

In order to benefit from a Mutual Check-*IN* both you and your partner should feel confident that you can understand, accept and practice the first three building blocks: Mutual Consent, Safety and Self-care. It is important for each of you to establish an informed consent regarding the depth of information you can reveal when relating to potentially hurtful behavior. For example, if your partner is troubled by fears of economic insecurity, it would be uncaring to leap into a conversation about your dissatisfaction with your job and your growing desire to quit.

Additionally, if either of you senses your safety is threatened during the Check-*IN* your focus must shift immediately to reducing that perceived threat. This is done using the steps previously agreed upon in your Safety Plans.

If the couple repeatedly gets bogged down in the material under exploration, it should be tabled until outside consultation can be obtained from a trusted professional or well-informed confidant. We offer you the following LOL, which provides guidelines to follow when you and your partner are conducting Mutual Check-*IN*s.

LOL
Mutual Check-*IN*

We suggest you consider the following when using our model for conducting Mutual Check-*IN*s.

- Read out loud from an agreed-upon source of spiritual or inspirational material to set the tone for the experience
- Share a prayer or a brief reflection related to the material that was read
- Take turns relating sources of discomfort that occurred during the day or week that felt like physical, emotional or spiritual challenges
- Identify with each other's challenges wherever possible.
- Share what you used to address the challenges, the outcome, and the plan for following up on issues raised
- Get input from each other about the challenges faced, strategies employed and the plan for follow-up
- Share what each of you is specifically grateful for today
- Share plans for maintaining physical, emotional and spiritual health until the next planned Check-*IN*
- Close with a prayer or shared moment of quiet meditation

Reciprocal INput

....

The third tool that couples have found useful in promoting Emotional Bonding is Reciprocal INput. The two of us learned that we both had some pretty big blind spots in our self-awareness, which made it difficult to maintain personal accountability. The firm and loving support we learned to provide as mutual accountability partners eventually revealed patterns in our behavior. We saw that, as we began to rely on and trust each other, the behavior became self-destructive and harmful to our romantic relationship. Unfortunately, the lessons came to us painfully slow. We hurt ourselves and each other a great deal before we became willing to give and receive input. It has not become natural or automatic for either for us to do, but we know today it is the easier, softer way to promote our romantic health.

The idea of giving or receiving input can feel pretty uncomfortable or even threatening, depending on what you have experienced in the past. Folks who grew up always being blamed for something – contrived or real – are apt to struggle with having their blind spots exposed. Likewise, children raised to be "seen and not heard" will most likely avoid giving input to others, especially to those they love.

When someone is bringing bad or unwanted news the easy thing to do is to "kill the messenger." It is not acceptable to exterminate people or cut them out of your life; however, death by character assassination or the dreaded "silent treatment" can be almost as bad.

Some people even struggle with input most others consider positive and harmless, like: "You are someone whose opinion I really value and trust." If you are someone whose life experiences taught you that positive input is too good to be true, then you will anxiously await for the bad news to follow. A child quickly learns to expect bad news when they hear, "you have done a good job pulling up your grades this semester, BUT…"

Input is intended to be constructive

Input should not be used to teach your partner a lesson or deflate their ego. Giving input is not like giving out a summons for a traffic violation. Remember you are providing the input because you care for them, not because you caught them misbehaving or you feel it's your responsibility to enforce some code of conduct. There are already far too many "behavior police" in our lives, running around looking for opportunities to let others know that they are "doing it all wrong."

It is vital to never give input under duress. If you do not feel safe, then do not do it. If you do not believe your romantic partner wants to see what you see, then do not do it. When you give people input under these circumstances, things may not go so well. Think about what happens in a fairytale familiar to most of us.

The witch in the fairytale asks her mirror to tell her who the fairest is in all the land. Unfortunately for the mirror, the witch has imposed a curse requiring it to always tell the truth. One day, the mirror tells the witch someone else is fairer than she. The witch becomes enraged. She smashes the mirror for telling her the truth and puts a plan in motion for the fairest one to be killed.

Critical ingredients

While we are not sure it would have helped the mirror any, it is critical when giving input for you to be prepared to share your experience, strength and hope with your partner, if he or she is willing to hear it.

If you are not prepared to share yourself with your partner, then your input is probably not going to be used in the way that you had hoped. We would also wonder what was motivating your desire to give your partner input. Are you trying to help or to control the other person?

When you share how you identify with what you see in your partner, you are using your experience to help your partner not feel judged by you. They are not likely to believe you think yourself superior to them when you share your personal experience as well.

Even if your partner is not prepared to reach out to you for help with the issue you have identified, they will be able to derive strength knowing you have been through the same thing, or are currently working on it. Your partner is less likely to feel all alone in it.

When couples are able to share so honestly with each other and work through vulnerable moments, a sense of hope in a mutually rewarding future will intensify.

The following guidelines are suggested as a way for you and your partner to provide and receive input to and from each other:

Providing INput

- Do not offer input if you are angry with or feeling threatened by your partner or when either of you have been using any mind or mood altering substances.
- Do not offer input if your partner has to agree with you — after all it is only your perception and not necessarily the truth.
- Provide your partner with an agenda of issues or events you would like to address through your input before asking for your partner's consent.
- Remain at eye level with your partner and allow him or her to control the volume of your delivery and the language you use (please no vulgarity).
- Keep your input focused on current or recent events and if you find yourself retrieving evidence from the past to support your current position, it is a good idea to stop giving input.
- If you find that you are repeating yourself, you are probably becoming fearful and it would be wise to stop the exchange.
- If your partner seems to be responding defensively, then the consent that you received has probably dissolved and you should stop for the time being.
- If you have noticed that your partner is now sharing his or her own concern for the issues you have

addressed, it is a pretty good indication that it is time to move from input to mutual sharing.

- The input you offer should be held as sacred. Never bring it up in an argument at a later time or you are not likely to get permission again for input any time soon.
- Be gracious and extend your gratitude for being heard regardless of whether or not your input leads to Mutual Support.

Receiving INput

- Do not consent to receive input if you are angry with or feeling threatened by your partner or if you or your partner is using any mind or mood altering substances.
- Do not agree to receive input if your partner seems to need you to agree with him or her, or if you know that you do not want to talk about the items on the agenda.
- Make sure you understand what issues your partner has on the agenda to discuss and do not agree if you really do not want input.
- You are free to set the conditions under which you will receive input.
- If you find yourself preparing a rebuttal, you are no longer receiving input you can use for your benefit and it would be wise to stop the exchange.
- If you find yourself feeling attacked, either re-state or redefine the conditions under which you will receive input or stop the exchange.
- If you find yourself waiting your turn, then your receiver has probably switched off. You do not have a turn coming. Either recommit to your consent to receive input or stop the exchange.

- Do not use the exchange as an opportunity to give your partner input that you have been avoiding even if you offer it with the intent of being helpful. If you have concerns about your partner save it for another time.

- If you do not have any questions for the purpose of clarification, you can offer to share what you discovered in your self-examination and move on to Mutual Support or just share your gratitude for your partner taking the risk.

- If you move on to Mutual Support, your partner may offer to share his or her experience, strength and hope and, while it can very often be extremely helpful, it is not wise to accept it if you are feeling overwhelmed.

Daily Connection

The fourth fundamental tool to consider when developing a lasting emotional bond is the need for Daily Connection. Most couples who come to us have spent so little time developing trust and communication that a few quality contact times each month or week is not sufficient to build the trust they need to be members of each other's support system. Most relationships need daily infusions of understanding, compassion, identification, nurturing and spiritual connection to build or sustain a healthy romance.

In order for your work in this book to produce the results that you desire, you and your partner need to make regular investments. All too often the relationships of the couples we meet are in trouble because the couple have either failed to nurture it, or allowed it to suffer too many periods of under-nourishment.

Simply putting aside one night a week to focus on a relationship actually gives some partners license to spend the remainder of the week totally preoccupied with work, independent hobbies or interests, chores around the house, the pursuit of personal down time, the steady stream of their children's extracurricular activities, and community projects. We often see romantic nurturance decline in relationships when the partners pick a weekly block of time to focus on their needs as a couple.

George and Jane

We had not heard from George and Jane for several years. Our work with them ten years earlier had helped them to navigate a terribly difficult time in their relationship when the death of one of their children had sent them spiraling into a very dark place. They came to trust each other with their pain and learned to run toward each other rather than away. They replaced a seemingly forced dependence on each other with the building blocks we have described so far.

Then came a crisis call from Jane. She and George had been steadily drifting apart during the past year. Both were talking openly about the boredom they felt in the marriage, and neither was sure they wanted to continue. One day Jane sat alone in a meditation time that had once been a Daily Connection shared with George, and picked up a dog-eared copy of our meditation course. It reminded her of the connection they once shared as members of each other's support system. She recalled the principle that couples don't fall out of love; they fail to work at being *IN* Love, and picked up the phone to call us for more help.

After six sessions we supported their decision to end therapy because they were willingly working to re-establish principles imbedded in the building blocks of Mutual Consent, Safety, Self-care and Emotional Bonding that they had constructed in their previous work in the marriage. They are currently working to regain the trust that they once relied on and are investing several hours per day in their relationship. The talk of divorce has evaporated in the heat of the romantic passion that they have been developing. They are working every day to enhance connection.

We encourage all of our couples to invest in their relationship on a daily basis. Most complain about the lack of time. Some question whether the two of them have enough to say to each other, and all acknowledge a fear that the intimate communication will leave them fighting every day. It is all right to be afraid, doubtful and confused. The list can and does go on and on. It is sad to hear couples present a barrage of obstacles to investing time into their relationship, especially when we have been asked to prescribe strategies for igniting the romance. There are times when our response to the presentation of excuses is seen as insensitive and antagonistic, but generally our answer to a challenge from the partner that they "do not have the luxury of working on the relationship everyday" because they "have too much to do" is – NOPE. You have all the time you need to make the relationship a priority. Give it the time it needs or you might end up giving it up and remember romantic relationships become sanctuaries when they are places of Mutual Support and intimate positive regard.

If you have made it this far in the book, then you and your partner have probably already begun to feel an enhancement of your emotional bond with each other. If the material has stoked the romantic embers we have introduced you to, we are thrilled but hope that you do not stop there. We have found that the glow of passion will fade quickly without regular attention.

The greeting card folks will promote the idea that we can send a gift that says it all when we find ourselves constantly on the run and not able to take the time to nurture a romance. We do not think a healthy romance can be sustained with cards and cute mementos but our position does not appear to be as widely accepted as theirs. The research of one leading company reports that 141 million Valentine's Day cards are exchanged annually, which suggests that there are more people listening to them then we have listening to us. We will never compete with the greeting card industry but we are currently working on a project that will provide a library of free strategies to guests at our website, www.leademcounseling.com, to aid you and your partner in your efforts to connect on a daily basis. In the meantime, we would like to offer you a favorite LOL of ours we call 5^2 (5 to the Couple Power).

LOL
5² (Couple)

The following exercise is intended to be used daily for the purpose of promoting *Mutual Support* and *Shared Accountability* and will only require that you and your partner find 25 minutes a day for yourselves. 5^2 (5^2 or Couple Power = 25 minutes) – isn't that cute.

The twenty-five minutes that you and your partner invest in this simple bonding exercise is not likely to over-burden your already demanding schedule. In fact, we have found it so rewarding that we have allowed it to expand, at times, for over an hour. We have found that it is a great way to begin our day so it is generally the first thing we do about 5:10 am every morning. We hope that it can become a regular part of your romantic diet.

1. Select a spiritual or inspirational reading of your choice and spend 5 minutes reading it out loud to each other. You are apt to find the daily meditations from *One in the Spirit: A Meditation Course for Recovering Couples* a great fit, but you are free to use any material you like as long as you both agree to it.

2. Sit quietly following the reading and reflect silently on what you have received for 5 minutes.

3. Write for 5 minutes about what the reading says to you and how you believe you might benefit from it.

4. When the writing time is up, spend the next 10 minutes with each partner having 5 minutes each to read out loud what he or she has written to his or her partner.

Closing

We are thrilled to have had the opportunity to share our passion for romantic health with you. It would have been a privilege to introduce you to the awakening process from the comfort of your living room but we did not get an invitation, LOL (Laugh Out Loud). Our dream is to one day have a homey facility to welcome you and other couples to share the journey toward romantic intimacy.

If you need us, please feel free to call. We would be glad to chat about your personal challenges to being *IN*.

~ Elaine & John ~

Made in the USA
Charleston, SC
11 February 2015